# AMERICAN BORN

# AMERICAN BORN

## BORN

An Immigrant's Story,
A Daughter's Memoir

Rachel M. Brownstein

The University of Chicago Press
CHICAGO & LONDON

The University of Chicago Press, Chicago 60637
The University of Chicago Press, Ltd., London
© 2023 by The University of Chicago

Published 2023
Printed in the United States of America

32 31 30 29 28 27 26 25 24 23    1 2 3 4 5

ISBN-13: 978-0-226-82306-5 (cloth)
ISBN-13: 978-0-226-82307-2 (e-book)
DOI: https://doi.org/10.7208/chicago/9780226823072.001.0001

Library of Congress Cataloging-in-Publication Data

Names: Brownstein, Rachel M., author.
Title: American born : an immigrant's story, a daughter's memoir /
Rachel M. Brownstein.
Description: Chicago, IL : The University of Chicago Press, 2023. |
Includes bibliographical references.
Identifiers: LCCN 2022010460 | ISBN 9780226823065 (cloth) |
ISBN 9780226823072 (ebook)
Subjects: LCSH: Mayer, Rose, 1905– | Jewish women—New York
(State)—New York—Biography. | Jewish women—Poland—
Biography. | Women immigrants—United States—Biography.
Classification: LCC F128.9.J5 B76 2023 | DDC 305.48/89240092 [B]—
dc23/eng/20220310
LC record available at https://lccn.loc.gov/2022010460

♾ This paper meets the requirements of ANSI/NISO Z39.48-1992
(Permanence of Paper).

# CONTENTS

Grandma Rose (1982). Photograph: © Xavier Lambours

# PREFACE

In the photograph my white-haired mother, seventy-seven years old, handsome, and still plump, by then a widow for four years, sits in a chair in a corner of my living room on Riverside Drive. A modernistic lamp with a translucent plastic shade lights her from above; houseplants crowd the darkness around her. She looks up and out, leaning her head on her hand, but her focus is inward: she is pensive, subdued, maybe a little melancholy but alert. The plants are gone now and the lampshade as well, but the comfortable chair—reupholstered—is still there in that corner of my living room. Six years older now than she was then, I sit in it often, these days, reading or just musing, like my mother. Often *about* my mother. For what this photograph suggests seems to me now to be true: if you have the privilege of watching your life wind up—or is it down—you tend to think about the shape of it, what it might have meant—or, as my mother would have put it, what it amounted to.

The portrait of my mother is signed and dated on the back, "06-82, souvenir from New York. Xavier." The French photographer was one of my husband's favorite kinds of finds, a lost boy, an artist, a natural surrealist, a stray to be nurtured by family life and my mother's chicken soup and by his own psychoanalyst's insights, free of charge. We had met Xavier in Paris; now he was visiting New York, collecting *souvenirs*,

French for memories. Rereading the inscription on the back of the photo, I think my mother would be pleased that a young French tourist should count a picture of her among his memories of her city.

One of the stories she liked to repeat to her children and grandchildren was about walking around a street corner, one afternoon, just in time to hear one neighbor remark to another, "With due respect for Mrs. Mayer," evidently preparing to say something not very nice about her. That would have been during her busy years as a mother in Astoria, Queens, where we lived in a three-room ground-floor apartment when I was a child. I never quite got the point of that story, only the pleasure she took in the formal phrase and the honorific, which delighted her almost as much as having accidentally stoppered the gossip's mouth.

To this day I can picture the brisk and popular "Mrs. Mayer" of my childhood, corseted and upswept and red-lipsticked, a respectable or, as she preferred, in Yiddish, a *balebatish* woman: that is who she was in the 1940s and '50s, decades before she turned into my children's benign, philosophical, amusing Grandma Rose. Another anecdote she liked to tell on herself (and me) in her old age, delivered with a sly glint, was about overhearing a new friend of mine saying, "Rachel, I didn't know you had such a Jewish mother." Self-aware often to the point of self-caricature, she was consciously a variation on a type she might have invented if Gertrude Berg had not played Molly Goldberg on television.

But Gertrude Berg did play Molly Goldberg on television, back then—conceived, wrote, and performed the comic role of the matriarch of a rising American Jewish family—and in my early teens we watched *The Goldbergs* together as a family, in the knotty-pine-finished basement of our row house in

Kew Gardens Hills, a bit farther out in Queens. "Yoo-hoo, Mrs. Goldberg!" her neighbor sang out to begin the show (and my mother sang along with her), and Molly threw up her window to talk across the alley where the wash hung and we—my brother and I and our parents—laughed at the Jewish way Molly talked, as we had laughed at the actress Minerva Pious playing Mrs. Nussbaum on Fred Allen's radio show, *Allen's Alley*, which we had listened to earlier in our small apartment in Astoria.

I grew up in the Golden Age of American Jewish comedy broadcasts. Nourished by the success of the Marx Brothers in the movies, buoyed by the vaudeville of the Borscht Belt in the Catskills, it ran from Jack Benny, Eddie Cantor, Milton Berle, and George Burns (a distant cousin of my mother's) through Sid Caesar, Carl Reiner, and Mel Brooks, who did Jewish *shtick*— literally "piece"—for laughs. Known to be Jewish by Jews, recognizable as such by non-Jews, these performers made it funny instead of tragic to be a Yiddish-speaking immigrant from Europe, where the Jews had nearly been exterminated.

Mocking the foreign accents of many of her relatives and neighbors, my mother fairly convinced us she had no accent herself. Our father had a slight accent, she conceded, explaining that he was "a naturalized citizen." (Implicitly, in contrast, Citizen Rose was Nature itself.) She herself had maybe an inflection in English, an intonation. A lilt. In her later years, as her Yiddishisms increased, she kept her critical little distance from her immigrant peers. The stereotype of the Yiddishe Mama threatened to swallow her, but she eluded by recognizing, dancing with it. She performed authenticity—as well as expertise. And in truth she had none of the creepy secrecy and evasiveness of so many assimilating social-climbing American Jews we knew—and little of the hopeful heartiness of the left-wingers, and only a touch of the sentimentality of truly pious Jews. Unapologetic about who she was and where she came from, she was a righteous but not self-righteous woman—and funny. By the time Dan Greenburg's *How to Be a Jewish Mother* was published in 1964, she could have written it herself.

My parents' favorite actor was a local hero who made it in Hollywood, the not-too-Jewish Brooklyn boy Danny Kaye, who sang and danced and even fenced, and did all kinds of languages and accents, in the movies. We had an album of his seventy-eights, which we listened to together and memorized. He was so smart and blond and handsome that my parents doted on him as if he were another son—not that any son of theirs would be a professional comedian. Our parents had academic aspirations for us. My smart and blond and handsome brother and I were good students, and in time we both duly became college professors. But in a way we were, deep down, a family of comedians.

———

My "own" earliest memories are versions of the stories she told about little me. I was one of those impressionable children who flee the pressures of family life—the threatening crosscurrents of puzzling passions—into books. The more imaginative of these children tell stories to themselves; others, like me, stay shy of making things up, and dabble at the shore of the real, playing with words. The backs of cereal boxes absorbed all my attention, at breakfast. I learned to read early: my mother proudly recalled my surprising them in the car before I was three by pointing to the neon sign and reading it aloud: "Coca-Cola." I was good at school. I loved to read books, and to study my teachers and playmates and even people on the subway, figuring out what kinds of characters they were. I couldn't get enough of the rules and rituals of school: according to my mother, the first day she took me to P.S. 6 to kindergarten, while the other children cried and clung to their parents, I ran to sit on a small chair and play at a table, and happily waved goodbye to her. She always added when telling the story that in her excitement she tripped and cut her knee and was bleeding as she left the school building. I coolly went on to get a PhD in English literature, and I stayed in school long after most reasonable people had left it: I did not retire from teaching until I was about the age my mother is in Xavier's 1982 portrait.

My mother told us regretfully that she herself had left school after the fifth grade. That would have been in Europe, I understood, and I pressed her to figure out the exact equivalencies: how old she was when she started school and when she left, what she studied in which grade. She remembered learning the multiplication table and the important rivers of Poland, but she was vague about why she had been taken out of school, only shaking her head over having had to leave it so young when she had liked it so much, unwilling to blame anyone for why that had happened. She too was a great reader: she had read Dostoevsky and Walter Scott in Polish, and later, in English, she read Romain Rolland's popular *Jean-Christophe* and the best-sellers *Forever Amber* and *Gone With the Wind*, and George Eliot's *The Mill on the Floss*, and apparently even *Romola* (but she might only have seen the 1924 film, starring Lillian Gish). In her old age, during summers in Vermont, when I was reading Trollope's Palliser novels, she did too. She delighted in the wickedness and greed of clever Lizzie Eustace. "She's something, that Lizzie," she would say, shaking her head as she laid down the paperback of *The Eustace Diamonds*, using the tone she might take about some adventuress we had both met. She appreciated nuances and excesses of character, gossip about people she knew and didn't know. A chance encounter in the supermarket with one of her neighbors might set her going, later, about the oddities of the woman's second husband—did I know he was her second, maybe her third—or the funny thing that happened to her hairdresser. She was not one of those helplessly self-referential people who comfort or torment themselves with tales of other people's misfortunes or successes: with her, it was story for story's sake, for character's sake. She enjoyed the human comedy. "For what do we live," Mr. Bennet asks rhetorically in *Pride and Prejudice*, "but to make sport for our neighbours, and laugh at them in our turn?"

One of my mother's favorite Polish proverbs, in something of the same vein, goes "*Jak się nie pocieszysz, to się powiesisz*," which she translated as "If you don't make a joke of it, you'll go hang yourself." She was quoting her grandmother, who had quoted a philosophical Polish woodcutter she had befriended. It was, as it were, my mother's philosophy of life, and—although my children correctly inform me that I didn't recognize her as a philosopher until they grew up and did so— I unthinkingly inherited it.

She wanted me to go to school and college and graduate school because she didn't get to go. She wanted me to type and to play the piano beautifully. The last was an impossible dream, but I did manage to type my way through high school and college and graduate school, as we needed the money. None of this is remarkable. What is extraordinary, as I see it now, is that she was so eager for me to work after I married and had children. I think she reasonably feared my being bored and oppressed at home. But "work" was not her word to describe what I did. What she wanted was for me to read, to type, to go to school, to do something outside the house and get paid for it—something bookish and different from what she had done when she was raising children. She wanted me to go to business, as she put it—and to drive a car, as she had never learned to do. It was about independence and progress and about social class: I was supposed to be a lady. Once when she came upon me mopping a floor, she sat down and wept.

I must have felt my mother's support of my teaching and writing career, but for a long time I was not quite conscious of how much I depended upon it. Some years before Xavier took her picture, when my children were still young and my working life was in full swing, she and my father left our apartment earlier than usual, after a Sunday visit, so I could prepare for my class the next day, when she would return to babysit. In the elevator, she later recalled to me, he asked her angrily, in Yiddish, *"Un du lusst doss?"* ("And you allow this to go on?") His language made it clear that he thought he had no say in the matter, therefore no responsibility for it: as he saw it, my wrongheaded choice to work was all her fault, as she was the enabler. He was correct: she was. And she told me this story all those years later because she wanted me to know that.

But he was complicit in the larger project of encouraging my brother and me to be American intellectuals—people with higher things on their minds than getting and spending and eating and drinking, people who did not work for other people at menial jobs, people entitled to deploy the English language for their own purposes. He was as pleased as she was that my husband and I chose to live in Manhattan near Columbia University and not in Queens or Brooklyn, and that our book-lined living room looked so different from theirs, in which a mirrored wall pretended to double the space. He was prouder than he might admit to being that I rejected their maroon-and-gold china and fancy patterned silver plate in favor of modern Scandinavian ceramics and sleek stainless steel.

In the process of pleasing my parents by reading books and going to school and mingling with Jews (and *goyim*) who looked down on little people like them, I came to see many things very differently from the way my parents saw them. I began to think that my mother not only enjoyed gossip and stories and characters but also was aware of being, herself, a character, like a character in a novel like *The Eustace Diamonds*.

She had a sense of herself as not only an individual but also an interesting type. And her appreciation of this, I think, put her at a pleasant, comfortable remove from her social persona and context, a little distance rather like an ironic omniscient narrator's. For what do we live, indeed? Maybe also to tell stories, the stories of our lives?

———————

When we were all together in the car or sitting around the table after a festive meal, my mother would often sing (and I would sing along with her) a bittersweet Yiddish ballad that had been popular among American Jews in the twenties and thirties, "*Die Greene Kuzine.*" It tells the story of the singer's lively young "greenhorn" cousin, who arrives in New York from Europe with cheeks like red apples and little feet that begged themselves to dance, who jumps instead of walking and sings instead of talking but over the years becomes old and defeated, with dark patches under her pretty blue eyes. In one version of the song, she is ruined by a love affair with a married man, but in the original she comes to grief because she is overworked and underpaid for someone else's profit in a sweatshop, a millinery factory. While the story is sad, the music is happy and the rhymes are snappy, and singing and remembering the lyrics together made my mother and me both feel good. Beginning in her late teens, she herself had worked in a millinery factory in New York alongside other "girls," most of them recent immigrants from Europe: she always claimed she had loved the job and excelled at it, and all her stories about her life as a working girl were tales of triumph.

In the first stanzas of the song, when the pretty Kuzine is dancing and singing and finally finding work, the narrator comments, apropos of the cousin's fate, "*Aza leben oyf Co-*

*lumbusns medina!*," "May Columbus's land have a long life!" But after the Greene Kuzine is broken by her hard life, the refrain changes to: "*Aza mazel oyf Columbusns medina*," or, variously, "*Brennen zol Columbuses medina*" ("Good luck/bad luck to Columbus's land!" or "May Columbus's land burn up!"). When she sang the song, my mother never articulated the terrible wish that America should burn up: she would never suggest such a thing, any more than she would curse a person she loved. The rules of behavior for religious Jews include injunctions against saying aloud what might actually come to pass if and maybe because you said it: she liked to recall her devout, skinny grandfather Moishidle shaking his little fist and shrieking at someone in a trembling rage, in Yiddish, "I wish you eighty-eight good years!!" Antiphrasis, or saying one thing and meaning another, is a common rhetorical device in Yiddish; for traditional speakers of the language, *akht un akhtsik*—the number eighty-eight—has uncanny negative resonances. Yiddish irony, which often depends on the voice and body, can be as terrible as anything by Jonathan Swift: Groucho Marx inherited the tradition.

As I remember it, my mother sang emphatically at the end of the song, with both gusto and disgust, "*Aza mazel oyf Columbusns medina*"—literally, good luck to America, as in "Goodbye and good luck," implicitly-ironically blaming the Kuzine's bad luck on the land Columbus "discovered"—blaming her tragedy on America for not living up to people's expectations, not being the Golden Land it professed itself to be. The strange word "*Columbusns*" (the explorer's name in the possessive and also the dative case) pleases me because it sounds like a slap in the face: "Goodbye, Columbus," it effectively says, proleptically, years and years before Philip Roth, ending the story of the *Greene Kuzine* by saying good luck and meaning bad luck, ironically, as is often the habit, in Yiddish. And ending, along with it, both the song and the story of Jewish immigration to America, and the tall story—the big lie—of Columbus's *goldene medina*, or golden land, where everybody prospered. Some working girls' lives did not work out so well, the song acknowledges. Some immigrants to America fail. Some dreams do not come true.

Some people call *"Die Greene Kuzine"* a working-class protest song; certainly, it is a song of disillusionment. To my mind, the phrase *"Columbusns medina"* conjures a storied mythical place, the proper name turned improper to emphasize its limitations.

My mother herself was not, strictly speaking, a greenhorn. She used to say with pride, "I am American born." The phrase always sounded a bit off to me, slightly foreign, and awkward, and as if protesting too much. For her, it was a declaration about citizenship and status as well as birthplace. Also, it seems to me now, about talent. She was born an American the way another girl might be born a figure-skater.

Reisel Thaler drew her first breath on the Lower East Side of Manhattan in 1905. But when she was two years old her mother died, and her father returned with her to Mielec, in Galicia, which was then part of the Austro-Hungarian Empire and later in Poland. She grew up there with her religious grandparents, speaking Yiddish and a little Polish, until she went back to America by herself at nearly nineteen. All through those years she remained proudly conscious of being American: when her third-grade teacher had pulled down the big map to show the class where America was, she had blurted, "I was born there!," but the teacher hadn't believed her, and the other children had made fun of her at recess for saying such a thing.

During the terrible Trump years, as I alternated between feeling relieved that my mother didn't have to live through them and wondering what she would have said about the outrageous goings-on, I thought a lot about her ideal of America and more generally about migration and the existential stakes of national belonging. Also meanwhile thinking, as I always have done, about language and languages, and how they shape us. Grown old myself now, I often find myself recalling my mother's words and phrases, muttering, for instance, apropos of somebody's pretentious claim to arcane wisdom, "Algebra, algebra, deep, deep!," as she and my father used to do years ago, as a joke, mimicking an ignorant neighbor who had been overly impressed by her young son's homework.

In my childhood and her middle age, it was especially important to my mother to have been American born, which distinguished her from many of the people in her circle in New York and then in Florida, the Jews who had fled Eastern Europe just before the Holocaust and the pitiable others who had trailed in later. Some of them were her close relatives—although many of those had been murdered in Europe. She was glad to be more American than they were, having escaped in good time. As a poor orphan girl living with elderly rigid grandparents, she had appeared to be less lucky than the children around her, but to her mind her origin in America had made her secretly stronger and better. All her life she clung to the ideal of America the beautiful, its tolerance and fairness, its openness and inclusiveness, the land of opportunity for all—even a girl like her—where race and religion and rank and riches and sex and status did not determine what you could do and who you could be, or what you thought and said about other people or to them. During these recent years when the ideal of America has been contested and hollowed out, deformed and debased and shamelessly faked, I have had many reasons to think of her.

# CHAPTER 1

# COLUMBUSNS MEDINA

Boys and girls together, me and Mamie O'Rourke
Tripped the light fantastic on the sidewalks of New York.

"The Sidewalks of New York" (1894 song)

"I arrived in New York City on March 17, 1924. It was Saint Patrick's Day," I hear my mother say self-importantly in the living room of my apartment on a sunny day over half a century after that date. "My brother Sam met me at the pier."

She has agreed to tell the story of her life to her grandson Gabriel, and she is feeling a little like a movie star as he somehow records the words she speaks on a celluloid tape. Listening in from the kitchen, I can sense Gabriel's effort to imagine the scene of arrival from her point of view, squinting to see in his mind's eye what she would have seen that day, an immigrant girl from a backward land walking alone down the gangplank into a heaving sea of jostling men in fedoras and caps, as in an old black-and-white movie. Gabriel asks her, "How did you recognize Sam in the crowd? Was he wearing a straw hat?" In my son's eagerness he gets the season wrong—mid-March is too early for a straw hat—but although she had worked as a milliner, that's not the problem she notices. "*He* recognized *me*," she corrects him. It wasn't exactly that she saw herself as she'd been, in her day, as the object of the gaze: more like the life of the party, or the guest of honor. The protagonist. The star.

Now I wonder: when she said Sam recognized her, could she have been telling Gabriel the simple truth? Could Sam actually have picked her out of the crowd coming off the ship as his nine-years-younger sister Reisel, whom he had last seen playing with a rolling pin beside the oven in their grandmother's bakery in Mielec, when she was seven or eight? Could be. In English, one of my mother's favorite Yiddish maxims, delivered in marveling tones, goes, "At seventy just like at seven." At eighteen-and-a-half, according to her passport, in fact a month before her nineteenth birthday, Reisel Thaler probably did have the same energetic, upright carriage, the regular features and level gaze, that she had had as a little girl and retained as the eager old woman so pleased to be interviewed by her grandson nearly seventy years later. The old woman trying to convey to Gabriel that it was her brother Sam's job and his duty to recognize and greet and welcome her, to serve as her protector in New York.

Maybe Sam had seen the snapshot her cousin had taken on the snowy day she had left Mielec for good, wearing a long white scarf and the navy-blue winter coat she had bought with the bit of money her grandfather had impetuously slipped her ("nobody should know") on his deathbed. Maybe that photograph had arrived from Mielec before she did, and had been delivered to Sam Thaler's place on Duane Street, on the Lower East Side, a day or so before the St. Patrick's Day when the *President Roosevelt* docked on the other side, the west side, of Manhattan Island.

In any case, what she meant to suggest was that the long shot Gabriel was projecting in his head, of the young immigrant Reisel striding bravely into a new world, had to be followed by a reverse shot: her story was not so much about the things she saw as it was about her way of seeing things, her point of view. And among the things she saw was herself being seen from other people's viewpoints. The way people saw her and how she looked back at them was the substance and the story of her life, as she recalled it. So savor the scene on the Hudson River pier on March 17, 1924, when Reisel Thaler looked around and relished coming (back) to America, which she had a perfect right to do no matter what kind of new laws the government passed, no matter what strict quotas for certain immigrants they tried to justify. She was not the poor immigrant girl she looked like, but a citizen of the United States of America. The passport in the little straw bag she carried was legal proof of her entitlement, her birthright: she had been born nearly nineteen years earlier in America.

For her father had come to New York before her, and a little later her mother and her brother Sam had joined him as planned, and soon after that another brother, Yussele, had been born on Pitt Street and then Reisel herself was born on Broome Street.

---

It would have been around the turn of the century that Abraham Isaac (or Eisig) Thaler (in Hebrew Avraham Yitzchak after his grandfather, and like him called Ahzhe in Yiddish, in the family and the village) had voyaged to America alone, as many poor European family men, not only Jews, were doing at the time. To seek his fortune, as they say in folktales. For sure there wasn't much luck where he started out, in Galicia, a cold, river-ridden, muddy province of the Austro-Hungarian Empire that bordered on both Germany and Russia, where impoverished Polish-speaking peasants were nearly outnumbered by equally poor Romanians, Ruthenians, Austro-Germans, Roma, and Jews. Side by side, in late nineteenth-century Galicia, these heterogeneous peoples maintained their different costumes and customs, languages and religions; the latter included two kinds of Catholicism, one that did and one that did not recognize the Pope of Rome. The groups did uneasy business with one another, and the place was cosmopolitan in its way; the towns along the rivers and railroads (Mielec was a station stop) were not as provincial as English or French villages of the time. But the living, for most people, was not easy. There were seething fears, resentments, and rivalries among the peoples of Galicia, and different estimates of who was on top and who should be. Jews were tolerated in the Austro-Hungarian Empire, which had granted them civil rights in 1867, three years before Ahzhe Thaler was born. Many of them considered the emperor Franz Joseph, who insisted on fair treatment for Jews in the army, as their protector, and referred to him in Yiddish—jocularly, familiarly, fondly and/or ironically—as "Franz-Yussel." But antisemitism persisted in the emperor's domain, violently at times, and it was fomented among the warring nationalities by hostile politicians. In Mielec, proximity to Russia and marauding Cossacks was a serious threat. And economic forces conspired to urge many a poor Jew to move on or away.

Anxiety about the anticipated end of the century may not have been at the level it would reach a century later, before the millennium, but there was enough fear of impending changes to make all kinds of people question traditional beliefs and feel apprehensive about the future. While some proudly espoused and represented their families' rival religions, many called for religion itself to be replaced by secular scientific modernity. Railroads brought different groups together, and in the growing cities they bumped up against one another, often abrasively. All over Europe there were clashes, revolutions, and assassinations; there were anarchists and nationalists of all sorts, including Jewish nationalists of different stripes. The First Zionist Congress met in Basel in 1897. Zionists argued that the Jews, after all a Middle Eastern people, could be persuaded to travel back east to cultivate the desert and revive the biblical language of Hebrew; meanwhile other Jews were writing, publishing, and performing in a proud new literary Yiddish. And yet other dissatisfied Jews sought opportunity and assimilation and traveled west toward the sophisticated secular cities of Western Europe—Vienna, Paris, and London—and settled there.

And farther west, as well. Between 1881 and 1914, an estimated 380,000 Jews emigrated from the Habsburg territories to America. Most of them were from Galicia. Many of the poorest of these people settled close to one another on the Lower East Side of Manhattan, a crowded neighborhood more tolerant of cultural differences than Galicia was. Around the turn of the century, my maternal grandfather Ahzhe Thaler became one of them.

His mother was a baker and a pillar of the Orthodox Jewish community in Mielec, a medium-sized city closer to Krakow than to Lemberg or Lviv. His very religious father sat at home or in the synagogue all day, praying and studying Torah. Ahzhe himself was a good-looking fellow with no interest in either studying or working with his hands—and alongside his brutish brothers-in-law—in the family bakery, or anywhere else he could think of. He wasn't much of a scholar—or even a Jew, he sometimes thought. He had lately lazily married to please his parents, a girl with sharp features who had a little money, and she soon was pregnant—and what was there for him to do, then? Business, he figured vaguely, but there wasn't enough cash on hand to start a business, and no business eager to employ him. He walked around the muddy streets of Mielec—a striking young Jew, with his light eyes and full blond beard— looking at the dogs and the people and chatting with this one and that and dreaming of escape. His wife delivered the baby, a boy, and too soon after that yet another baby boy, and he was still walking around, doing a little of this and a little of that, going nowhere. His wife's brother, a congenial fellow he enjoyed playing cards with, went off to New York and sent home postcards that described, in the Yiddish language written in Hebrew characters, lively beach parties with pretty girls in bathing suits at Coney Island. They had a big amusement park there. And meanwhile handsome Ahzhe Thaler was still doing the same boring nothing. His family was growing and suffocating him; he had to get away.

Motives are obscure and mixed. Was Ahzhe's momentous move across the ocean a result of his personal fecklessness and failure to thrive, or was it the reflex of a wandering Jew— a would-be modern, bored-of-believing Jew? Did he intend, from the beginning, to send for his wife and their small sons, Chayim and Samuel, or did he travel abroad to escape them? Was permanent immigration to America—settling there— his aim? What about his wife's? Might his motives have been political as well as economic? Did he in fact have what you might call motives, or was he just looking around for money or a change, and doing what people he knew were doing then? I don't know the answers to these questions.

It was probably just before 1900 when Ahzhe stepped off the transatlantic steamer in New York. At some point after that he sent for the little family he had left behind in Europe. He might have managed on his own for two or three years before they showed up. When I try to imagine Ahzhe on the loose in New York, I don't see him crossing Delancey Street sporting the *peyes* and long beard, broad-brimmed hat, and traditional belted black satiny caftan of the Orthodox European Jew. He would have been a nattier figure than most, I think, watchful and curious; but I wonder how modern and secular he dared to be in the very beginning, or what he did for money in New

York. When his daughter, my mother, was born in 1905, he identified himself to the officials for her birth certificate as a "herring merchant"; in his middle age he would keep a fancy grocery store in Mielec that stocked imported delicacies. He seems to have worked all his life at selling food retail, as two of his sons would also do, in a small way, like him.

I wonder what he did for fun as a seemingly single man, early on, in New York. Did he continue to keep kosher, living in one or another of the many apartments that served as rooming houses for single immigrants on the Lower East Side? Did he tell people he was married? Did he flirt—he was famously a ladies' man—with the women he met on the ship, and with the newly American Jewish ladies, with wigs and without, whom he met in the shops on Delancey? A sociable sort, he would have known some people in the neighborhood from the old country, and some others would have known of him: "*Ritt un Pitt un Delancey in der mitt*," as they rhymed to show their familiarity with it, was the heart of a crowded Jewish neighborhood (Reade Street and Pitt Street and Delancey Street in the middle).

His surname, Thaler, meant dollar in German. Officials would have recorded his arrival at Ellis Island (est. 1892). In my childhood most of the family insisted on retaining the Yiddish pronunciation, *Toller*. But early in the twenty-first century, one of my grandfather's descendants, my first cousin's daughter, changed her first name to Thaler, pronounced *Thayler*. My mother always thought that pronunciation was "fancy," that is, pretentious and wrong.

———

It had by no means been original for Ahzhe Thaler to immigrate alone to America and send for the wife and children later. My paternal grandfather, the mild and modest Abra-

ham Chayim (always called Avrum Chayim) Mayer, who as it
happened hailed from the same Galician *shtetl*, also left his
wife and family and traveled to America alone, in his case just
before the First World War. Immigration to this country did
not begin to be restricted by law until 1921, so there was lots
of movement back and forth. As there were few social services
for new arrivals, Jews from the various towns and cities of Russia and Poland, following the example of German Jews, set up
fraternal associations to sustain and bury one another. It is
hard to conceive of how these people imagined their futures
and their social and civic relations, to one another and to the
*goyim* around them.

Ahzhe Thaler's wife's parents, poor people for all that their
daughter had come to him with a little dowry, were either living
in New York City when he got there or arrived soon afterward.
Or maybe they came along with their daughter and one of her
two children when Ahzhe finally sent for his wife. All I know
about them is that they did not help him when he was in need,
when his wife Shprintze died suddenly at forty and left him a
widower in New York with two young sons, a male infant, and
the tiny daughter who would become my mother, who had been
born two years earlier. Evidently, and shockingly, as it forever
seemed to my mother and still seems to me now, they did not
adopt any of the children.

———

My mother sketches this murky prehistory in her early nineties, not at all for the first time, sitting in a comfortable chair
on a sunny afternoon in my living room on Riverside Drive,
sharp as a tack and way more charming, sucking the sugared
coffee beans Gabriel has brought to soothe her throat, com-
placent about being old and beloved and flattered by being

formally interviewed by her handsome grandson, the writer. Although he questions her, she does not have much to say about her parents and their movements and motives, actual or imagined. In her old age my mother, like most of us, enjoyed nothing more than talking about herself.

Sketching her parents' story in broad strokes, she comments about her mother, with a little half-suppressed giggle you can still hear, "When she got to America, she begot, first Yussele and me and then Harry." The human voice, recorded, can make an absent person seem eerily present—especially if she's dead, and your mother. Replaying the tape now, I recognize her flirtatious playing up to Gabriel, her literary grandson, by playing cleverly with the English words "got" and "begot" (who knew she knew that archaic term?) to mock her mother a little for having so many children she didn't know what to do with. She explains that when her father Ahzhe summoned his wife Shprintze to join him in America she brought along Sam, the second of the first two Thaler boys, but was persuaded to leave Chayim, the older, at home in Mielec. "My grandmother didn't let Chayim go," she repeats proudly, on the tape. I register, not at all for the first time, my mother's admiration of her beloved grandmother's stern righteousness, and her will and power—and my mother's sense that her own poor mother Shprintze (as well as her maternal grandmother) lacked those noble womanly qualities.

The Bubbe Brucha was Ahzhe's mother. A family tree drawn many years later indicates that she and her husband had had an older son who moved away to Germany, early on, but Ahzhe was the only male child remaining to them in Mielec. The Bubbe's legendary strength of mind and body was the basis of my mother's profound reflexive feminism, and I guess it is of my own feminism, as well. It didn't occur to either of us to blame Brucha for spoiling blue-eyed Ahzhe rotten.

Hearing her talk about the retention in Mielec of little Chayim when he was about ten, I have a flash of memory of my uncle Chayim as I knew him when I was a child, an old, strangely tentative foreign man with crooked wire-rimmed spectacles and a long messy white-and-black beard in which, we used to joke, he threaded the diamonds he smuggled into this country from Europe. I'm not sure when Chayim first came to America, or how many times he came and went back: an uneasy English speaker, he was the most old-world of my mother's four brothers, as her youngest brother Harry was the most worldly and American. Harry had been the baby abandoned in New York as a months-old infant after Shprintze died and Ahzhe returned to Mielec and deposited his little girl with his mother. While Reisel was growing up in the Bubbe Brucha's bakery in Mielec, her almost-two-years-younger brother Harry was living across the ocean in the Hebrew Home for Orphans in New York, where the children's clothes had no pockets. When Harry and Reisel first met in New York in 1924, they lacked a common language, as he spoke only English and she spoke Yiddish, mainly. Harry saw Europe for the first time in his prosperous middle age, when he took an ocean liner to Italy on a honeymoon with his American-born wife, the daughter of a wealthy Jewish plumber.

There were to be two sets of children in Ahzhe's first family, one European (the older boys, Chayim and Sam) and the second increasingly American, in order of birth, Yussele, Reisel, and Harry. And then Ahzhe, back in Mielec, would sire a second daughter, Ruth or Roozha, with another wife, Paircha, who came to him with two daughters of her own—and he would effectively abandon his other children. There were to be separations and emigrations, and who knows how many alliances, rivalries, resentments, confusions, and boastful and invidious distinctions among these tensely connected people. What one wants to know is how they felt, what they were like and how they imagined their lives, which is hard now to recover.

"He wasn't so crazy about my mother," my own mother says flat-out about her father Ahzhe Thaler; "they married him off to her." Not a love match: you can hear the scorn in her voice, how much she disapproved of this unfortunate fact, being all for love, as well as consistently critical of her unfatherly father. My cousin Adrianne, whose mother was Ahzhe Thaler's daughter by his second wife, tells me her grandmother Paircha liked to recall the sexy moment when her eyes met Ahzhe's over the trays of wedding rings in the jewelry shop in Germany where she worked as a salesgirl, which is where she first met him: *coup de foudre* for both the widow and the widower, for the first time for both. Memory is at least as mysterious as desire. On Gabriel's recording, my mother describes all four of her brothers as crazy about her, as she was crazy about them—a claim I recall her making in my childhood. As a young person I had thought her claim was a self-serving and didactic lie, since the Thaler siblings had not grown up together as I was growing up with my only brother. I am less scornful now of what she said, and no more certain of what she meant by saying it.

Late in life, when she was given to making stunningly general moralizing pronouncements, my mother liked to point out that of all her brothers only Harry had had a good wife: the other women pushed the poor jerks around. "The dumbest woman is smarter than the smartest man" was one of her favorite maxims, and her intelligent husband had taught her—as if she hadn't figured it out herself—that her brothers were not so smart. She herself, as she saw it, was not only smart but the gold standard in wives, tactful and forbearing. There were those who disagreed with her.

About her feeling for my father, her husband, the only man she ever loved or even thought of, she always said what she says on the tape with shyly suggestive simplicity, which is what she always said to me when I was growing up: "I liked him," and "He liked me," both "Right away." In other words, *coup de foudre*. She tells Gabriel the story of how, soon after they first met as fellow boarders in the same apartment in New York, he had fixed her up on a date—perversely, or to test her? or to fool or test himself?—with a rich and eligible friend of his, a successful businessman who lived uptown on Riverside Drive, and then asked her to tell him what she thought of the guy. "I didn't like him," she said she told him, and so, as she put it, that was that: in other words, it signaled "I like you a whole lot better." She was a romantic—in that as in so many ways a hard act to follow.

<hr />

During some twenty years of hearing his grandmother's stories, Gabriel has learned the right comments to make and questions to ask: he feeds her the prompts for her greatest hits. For example, he says when she narrates her triumphant return to New York on her own, at nearly nineteen, on that cold bright day in 1924, "You didn't have to come in through Ellis Island, right?," and she responds with patriotic pride and vigor, "No, I was an American." It was important to her that the day she landed in New York was St. Patrick's Day, just as it would be important to Al Smith, then governor of New York and one of my mother's heroes, to begin construction of the Empire State Building on that Irish saint's day six years later, in 1930. The luck of the Irish was available to all in America, she hoped.

On principle, as an American, my mother enjoyed being ecumenical, and over the years, partly because she admired Al

Smith the working girl's champion, she came increasingly to favor the Irish. When my brother married, she was delighted by her daughter-in-law's Irish surname. For her, St. Patrick's Cathedral (along with the Reform Jewish Temple Emanu-El, also on Fifth Avenue, which important Jews like Governor Herbert H. Lehman attended) was the major monument to religion in the city. The immense Episcopal Cathedral of St. John the Divine uptown was not in her line of sight. Her brother Sam sent her a St. Patrick's Day card with a picture of a lucky shamrock on it every year until he died, to commemorate the event of her second coming. Growing up, my brother and I were dragged through the crowded streets and subways to the St. Patrick's Day parade on Fifth Avenue every year. I remember wearing my Kelly-green "topper" (a short coat my father said made me look green), and the drunks vomiting on the subway platforms.

On Wikipedia I discover that 1924, the year my mother came back to America, was also the year of the first Macy's Thanksgiving Day parade: we never missed one of those, either.

My mother loved a parade, and her healthy respect for Macy's was analogous to my father's awe of General Motors. My father bought a series of mid-range General Motors cars, over the years, and eventually some General Motors stock; he believed the capitalist credo that what was good for General Motors was good for the nation. My mother, in turn, admired the success and amazing variety of Macy's Department Store. While both my parents voted Democratic, my mother the populist—a Zionist socialist in her youth—not only loved Al Smith but voted for Henry Wallace. If she remained a little to the left of my father, they both had faith in the economic system that had enabled America to get rich and defeat the Nazis and win the war. And, like most American Jews then, both of them believed in the wisdom and grace of Hitler's aristocratic enemy, Franklin Delano Roosevelt.

My mother's admiration of Macy's was partly rooted in her career as a milliner: Macy's had pretty much called the shots, in the 1920s, in the millinery trade. The big store sold more ladies' hats than any other retail store, and thus it effectively, along with Hollywood, created the craftily shifting fashions in headgear. Even though she always made a traditional turkey dinner for Thanksgiving, an American seder complete with sweet potato casserole to which she invited stray male relatives who had no one to cook for them, she always also managed to take us by subway in the morning to admire the big floats and the costumed marching bands in Macy's Thanksgiving Day parade. She delighted in pointing out the dignitaries as they passed, and recalling, for instance, that Mayor LaGuardia's mother was Jewish.

She boasted all her life that she had been in the crowd at Lindbergh's ticker-tape parade on Fifth Avenue, and she stubbornly refused to give credence to the well-founded rumor that the aviator hero had sympathized with Hitler. "Lucky Lindy" was one of the old songs she loved to sing—to perform—for us. An enthusiastic singer with a clear mezzo-soprano, she liked to belt out "I . . . love a parade." Partly because she dragged us to so many of them, my brother and I did not.

---

If you look at it hard enough from some perspective, every year is a banner year. The chronicle of a single year has become a popular genre of cultural history—not only famous years like 1848 and 1968 but obscure ones like 1873, 1912, 1948. Bill Goldstein's *The World Broke in Two: Virginia Woolf, T. S. Eliot, D. H. Lawrence, E. M. Forster, and the Year That Changed Liter-*

*ature* (2017) argues, for instance, for the importance of a year two years before the one when my mother's life story broke into its two parts, sinister European and sunny American.

Writing almost a hundred years later, as my parents' daughter and an old woman myself, I could make a case for 1924 as the year that changed everything for Reisel Thaler, who would become Rose Mayer. Like 1922, it was a notable year for modernism: in February 1924, the month before my mother arrived in New York, George Gershwin's "Rhapsody in Blue," which altered "classical" music by making it jazz-ily American, had its premiere in that city. Also in 1924—on June 9, almost four months after Reisel disembarked into the arms of her brother Sam—a dark-eyed young man, also from Mielec, whom Reisel had never met there, received his final diploma from the *Hochschule fur Welthandeln* in Vienna—he would preserve the precious papers in a leatherette folder all his life—and set off on the second leg of his own voyage west-ward. Another Yussel, like Reisel's brother and one of her close cousins and in a sense the Kaiser himself, he had been born in 1898 to a couple in the same poor observant Jewish community as Ahzhe Thaler's family. On Friday afternoons, his younger brother had brought to the Thaler bakery oven their mother's *cholent*, a stew of beef, beans, barley, and potatoes that cooked for twelve hours together with other neighbors' kosher cas-seroles, to be eaten after the Sabbath on Saturday night. The *Shabbes goy* employed in the bakery, not subject to Jewish law and therefore permitted to work on the Sabbath, kept the fire going from sunset on Friday to sunset on Saturday so that the whole community could comfortably enjoy their hot dinners without actively cooking. But this Yussel had never had any-thing to do with the bakery or other household matters.

I am not at all sure that my father had New York City in mind as a destination when he left Mielec for Vienna as soon as he could after the end of World War I: I rather think he dreamed of settling in Austria's cultural center. Beginning with his notable absence from the Bubbe Brucha's bakery on Fridays, his life story as I know it is full of holes. The only anecdote I have about his childhood came to me through my storytelling mother: his family was very poor, she recalled, and once, as his mother finished patching a hole in her small son's torn trousers, she examined her handiwork with satisfaction and proudly pronounced it "*a latteleh azoy vie bai'em Kaiser*," a patch like they make in the Kaiser's house. The story is a little poem of Yiddish irony, irony that trumps poverty and patches and (ruefully) even pride in a good piece of work. Like the snobbish, superior-looking shoemaker in a short story by the Yiddish writer Avrom Reisin, who doesn't make shoes but only patches them, my grandmother Rochl saw herself ruefully as a *latutnik*, a maker of patches: her work was to patch up a bad business. The uses of irony are multiple: the further it could take you from your own life, the better off you were, in the lost world of our fathers and mothers.

Remarkably, in the cloistered, tradition-bound world of European Orthodox Jews, it was possible for an intellectually promising young male to rise in social and economic status. Because the study of Torah was the supreme Jewish value, the poorest of bookish boys had a chance to achieve distinction and to radically improve on his family's position. If he was a smart boy, he could become a rabbi and a sage. The story goes that my father was so intellectually promising so early that at the age of only three he was seated under the table at the Hebrew school or *cheder* to feed, as it were, on the crumbs dropped down by the rabbi and the older boys.

I have no idea whether that table stood in the two-towered stone *Beth ha-Midrash* in Mielec that opened its doors in 1902—the year my father turned three—or in a humbler *shti-*

*bel* or small *shul* frequented by poor people: I suspect the latter. That he studied so well and learned so fast was the central and defining fact of Yussel's life: everything paled in the radiance of his great gift. More solidly than a rich man or a doctor or even the Kaiser himself, a boy like him in a place like Mielec was considered intrinsically better than other people, and therefore was excused to sit out ordinary domestic life. His brother was the one who helped their ailing mother to keep the household running after their father left for America: Yussel's only obligation, to his family as well as to God, was to sit and study Torah. That was all he studied: he was never registered in a secular school, never taught multiplication or division or the names of European rivers, as my mother had been. But curiosity and respect for learning and the habit of study led him eventually to read non-holy books on his own: like Thomas Hardy's Jude the Obscure, he became an autodidact.

That a grand synagogue with two towers got built in Mielec in 1902 suggests that the city's Jews were numerous and prosperous enough then to encourage them to build so high, and that they intended to continue to prosper in a society dominated by Christians and, increasingly, people who rejected religion. My father's early life, like my mother's, was situated within the world of the Kaiser and his people but also simultaneously at a great social and spiritual remove from it. For Orthodox Jews like their families, regular daily prayers and a weekly Sabbath holiday in addition to religious festivals with their peculiar traditional customs and ceremonies throughout the year, along with the six hundred thirteen commandments regulating daily life, determined everything one did, therefore who one was.

The Jews were a people apart: they kept themselves apart from others, with their special food and clothing and ceremonies, and Christians stayed separate from them. Most Eastern European Jews did not adopt and pass down surnames until the nineteenth century. On the documents he saved from the school in Vienna, my father's last name is given as Steuer, his mother's family's name, rather than his father's, which was Mayer. Had his parents been married according to the law of the land they lived in? A punitively high tax on Jewish marriages had been established in 1773, and they were poor people: possibly, their religious marriage had never been officially registered with the state. I am far from sure of the circumstances in this case, but I suspect that many religious Jewish couples regularly failed to register their marriages and births, feeling as they did more comfortable (if that is the word) on the margins of the Empire. Maybe there was some notion of avoiding a military draft, as well. I don't know exactly what the facts were. Nor do I know what provoked young Yussel Steuer or Mayer to break, or try to break, with the exclusively Jewish life he knew, which he did at some point during or around World War I. But about that I have some idea.

When my brother began reading philosophy at Columbia College at only fifteen, our father related a version of a conversion story to him. One day, in or around the outhouse behind the *cheder*, he and some friends came upon a copy of a book by or about the philosopher Spinoza, a book in Yiddish that changed his life. Through the modern media of translation, print, and railways, the seventeenth-century Spanish Portuguese philosopher educated in the *cheder* of Amsterdam spoke directly to the *yeshiva bocher* trapped in early twentieth-century Jewish Mielec. What Spinoza's philosophy suggested was, in effect, that for a seeker after truth a *cheder* was not a promising place to be.

Exactly what prompted my father's spiritual upheaval and/or intellectual ambition is not clear to me: I don't know whether the book was in fact by Spinoza or about him, and which book it was. Was it a journalist's introduction to works of the early modern renegade Jew who had been excommunicated by the rabbis of Amsterdam? From Google I learn that precisely such a book, by S. Y. Stupinski, was published in Warsaw around 1915. Had the volume been left behind in the privy by a secret freethinker, accidentally or in an effort to conceal it, or was it deliberately placed there to tempt the studious boys?

The hormones of adolescence, the rumors and fears of a coming war, the mud and the cold, the poverty and patches and the tedium must have helped. The important Jewish philosopher's words, however simplified and vulgarized, spoke directly to the boy and changed his life. However distorted, the voice of Baruch or Benedictus Spinoza, valued by Christian thinkers and condemned by the rabbis of Amsterdam, pierced the synagogue chants that filled Yussel Steuer's ears. There was a kind of logic to it: he was in the habit of taking instruction from a book, and he was ready, as well, to discover the natural world in which, Spinoza argued, God lives and moves. Yussel resolved to leave dark and backward Mielec for Vienna, the cultural capital, hoping to study further. Somehow, he already knew or knew of men who had done that. He had to wait till the war was over—by which time, I think, his mother must have died, and his younger brother would have left to join their father in America.

It is a secondhand story, transmitted by father to son and then, much later, from my brother to me. It is, as I said, full of holes, mostly about dates (his father's departure from Mielec and his own and his brother's; his mother's death) and about money, but also about books and translations, teachers, and friends. How and where did Yussel learn to read German? Was there a stray renegade Jew in Mielec who advised him to take a particular correspondence course? Could Yussel have been the only Jewish boy in Mielec who decided to escape? Had he spent the war effectively underground, hiding from the draft? How did he prepare himself for classes in German? And when did he stop putting on his *tallis* and *tefillin* to pray every morning, which I remember him doing daily—having resumed the traditional pious habit—when I was a child? Like my mother but in a different key, my father was obsessed by Jewishness and conflicted about it all his life. He tried to lapse but failed. Unlike the resolutely optimistic woman he married, he became, as a result, a serious skeptic, dubious and pessimistic.

In the new school for world business in Vienna he attended— it was established the same year as the League of Nations—he would have studied some French and German as well as business arithmetic. In 1924, when he had to drop out because his father stopped sending him money, there was no question, for him, of going back to Mielec. Nor would recent American law permit him to immigrate to New York, where his father lived. Instead, he traveled westward to Paris—the capital of the nineteenth century, the center of the Enlightenment, the city of light—as he described it to me and I, a sleepless child, lulled myself with mental pictures of light reflected on the glamorous ripples of the river Seine at night. A wealthy family of Mielecer Jews he knew had a factory in Paris, and he got a job there.

Like Vienna, Paris was a mecca then for Eastern Europeans searching for a new secular way of life. In 1905, the year my mother was born in New York, the French passed a law definitively separating church and state. My father's contemporary, the Galitzianer novelist and journalist Joseph Roth, wrote eloquently about what a wandering Jew might find to love about Paris in the 1920s, for all the problems posed by the pronunciation of French vowels and consonants. He details an interesting little list: the French indulgence for arguments about ideas, in loud voices, on the streets and in the cafes; those charming civilized cafes themselves, where you could sit for hours as waiters piled up the little plates you paid for only when you left for the day; the more dimly lit places near Montmartre where for a few francs a man could dance with his choice of blonde or even brown-skinned *shiksas*; the superior food and drink. Paris was at the center of the Enlightenment. When my father got there, the friend he had known and loved since *cheder* welcomed him into his family's feather business (pillows, duvets), and he set about to explore and enjoy the historic city. He had enjoyed the romance of Vienna, and years later he told us stories about student duels and facial scars—borrowed perhaps from the pages of Stefan Zweig—and taught us to sing the Latin student drinking song, *"Gaudeamus igitur,"* as if he himself had sung it together with other young men in beer gardens. Paris was similarly redolent of romance.

He loved the beautiful city and the French language, but he remained dissatisfied with himself. Some men lived for pleasure, and although intellectually he approved of that, he himself was not one of those men. In Vienna, in the first flush of his excitement about Western culture, he had tried out alternative identities, wearing a monocle in his eye and carrying a cane to second-act operas, and even bearing a spear, once, as an extra in a crowd scene for a movie. But now he was getting older and thinking about the future. He asked his employer, his friend P.'s uncle, for suggestions about what more he might do in the business, or what he might seek elsewhere in the city, but nothing seemed possible or appetizing. The uncle suggested that things might be better for him in Montreal, Canada, where there was an outpost of the family's business—another factory or a store—in the Bonsecours Market. His conversational French was passable. He might travel across the Atlantic as if on a business trip. If things didn't work out for him in Montreal, who knows? It was not far from there to New York, where there were more Mielecers.

Since the age of three he had been studying Jewish law, the Torah and the commentaries on it. His teachers had thought he would be a scholar, a rabbi. He had left Mielec wanting to know everything. Now he aspired to learn the laws of physics and economics, to study political economy—to be a lawyer, he imagined. In search of a course of study and eventually a profession, he found himself crossing the Atlantic on a Canadian ship, the SS *Chicago*, traveling from Bordeaux to Halifax in November 1927. On the ship's manifest he is listed as Joseph Steuer, a Hebrew from Galicia, a speaker of both French and German. His ticket said it had been purchased by J. P. of Paris, his employer. He is the only passenger on the list who is not classified as an immigrant. His journey might have been plausibly construed as a business trip. When asked, upon disembarking, for the address of his nearest relative, he gave the name of J. P. in Paris and then, as an afterthought (it is scribbled in the margin), the name of Abraham Mayer on Kaiserstrasse in Vienna. It was the only lie he told, but it was a big one, and telling: his father, who had never seen Vienna, was in fact living in New York.

Yussel must have taken the train with most of the other passengers from Halifax to Montreal. I don't know when or whether he checked in at the Bonsecours Market, or when or why he decided to leave Canada for New York. When he did so, he let them know he was coming, and they sent Reisel Thaler, the boarder, who knew her way around town, to meet him at the train station. She quickly picked him out as he stood on the platform at Grand Central Station, and just as quickly noticed that his fly was partly open. Of course she didn't mention it, how could she?

He had no passport, no visa, no identity cards—no papers

but those precious ones with ornate signatures that they had bestowed upon him at the business school in Vienna. He was literally a man without a country: Mielec had been a city in the Austro-Hungarian Empire when he was born there in 1898, but after the Armistice it was in Poland. He lacked any proof of legal citizenship either in the defunct empire or in Poland. The Immigration Acts that severely limited the entry of European Jews to the United States had been passed in 1921 and 1924: although he was a man quite literally compounded of laws, the law of the land his father had moved to was now directed, ironically, against him. Washed up on the Lower East Side of New York, he would be illegal. Nevertheless, on purpose or not, the student from Mielec found himself on his roundabout way to the only home he could stake a slight claim to, his father's apartment in that immigrant Jewish neighborhood. Bewildered in Halifax and then Montreal, where he knew nobody, he soon picked up his belongings—some clothes, a few books, and if he still had them, his phylacteries—and took the train south to New York City.

When with the help of his young lady guide he arrived at his father's house, he discovered that two female boarders were already in residence there. They were Mielecers both: his father's second wife's daughter Rivka and her good friend Reisel Thaler, the open-faced girl of striking self-confidence who had welcomed him to New York. The short, darkly handsome young man was a little older and a little taller than both girls— the tallest person in the household, at nearly five foot five—and he considered himself to be in every other way as well superior to these provincial, ignorant, superstitious people from the backward world he had fled. He moved in with the family— his father's family—as a son. He took his tasteless meals with The Mister and The Missus and the working girls who boarded with them. At some point he took his father's surname, Mayer.

It took him a while, but in the end, Reader, he married her, on February 26, 1933. And in the spring of 1937, some thirteen years after leaving Vienna for Paris, Josef or Joseph Steuer or Mayer, now of New York City—Yussel, they called him, like the good Kaiser Franz-Yussel—would become my father.

# CHAPTER 2

# CHARACTERS AND CHARACTER

Nothing so true as what you once let fall,
"Most Women have no Characters at all."
Matter too soft a lasting mark to bear,
And best distinguish'd by black, brown, or fair.

ALEXANDER POPE, "Epistle II: To a Lady,
Of the Characters of Women" (1735)

In 1905, the year my mother was born, there was a revolution in Russia. That same year Albert Einstein published his theory of relativity, and Franklin Delano Roosevelt, a cousin of the president of the United States, married his cousin Eleanor. (The ship that would bring my mother back to New York was named the *President Roosevelt* after the well-born couple's rough-riding cousin Theodore.) Variously understood, these famous Americans—Einstein and the Roosevelts—figured importantly in my mother's consciousness, her affective and moral life, as they did in the minds of so many American Jewish women and men of her generation. They were her heroes and paragons, model human beings, people whose example a person should strive to live up to.

To some extent our characters are informed by the portraits of characters we have in our heads. My mother's respect for her generous and just grandmother Brucha nourished her commitment to a nearly lost ideal of character—character as a lasting mark as opposed to a role, in Shakespeare's slippery phrase a "glassy essence." Her ideals of humanity and human-ness accorded well, in the 1920s and 1930s, with the prevailing picture of America, then: a place where a person's worth was not determined by her parentage or class.

———————

Repeated and revised in changing circumstances to different effect, my mother's favorite anecdotes, over the years, have become a collection of stories, maybe two sets like her moth-er's two sets of children, separated by the vast Atlantic. "What should we talk about? Mielec or America?" she asks Gabriel a little nervously at the beginning of the interview—trying to get oriented, maybe also to recall the way she herself had be-gun to write down her life story in Florida, ten years earlier. Her grandson defers to her, and she surprises him by choosing Mielec, the site of her first memory. "You were talking about the coat," Gabriel says. That would have been the new red coat or cape she accidentally tore on a nail when she was a little girl, I know.

There are several important coats in my mother's life story: the warm coat my father promised her in the proposal of mar-riage he made while walking over the brand-new Triborough Bridge, for example, when he told her that after she married him, if he needed a coat and she needed a coat she would be the one to get the coat; also the navy-blue coat she wore on the snowy day she left Mielec for America, a long coat she bought with the cash Moishidle secretly slipped her just before he died. It was cold most of the time where she grew up; poor people, old people, maybe all motherless children have trouble keeping warm. It is hard to know where to begin the story of a life, and I begin again here with my mother's beginning—

with her birth, that is, her first arrival in America—although
the dramatic scene of her coming back to New York, the great
good place where she had been lucky to be born, keeps trying
to take over.

The house she was born in on Broome Street—Ahzhe Thaler
and family had moved there from Pitt Street, where my
mother's next older brother Yussele had been born—would
have been a narrow tenement five to seven stories high, probably a brownstone with a flight of stone steps in front. (Edith
Wharton considered brownstone an especially ugly building
material.) I don't know whether my grandparents rented an
apartment or just a room or even half a room, curtained off,
in another family's apartment; the building would have been
razed years ago. All I was told was the story that one afternoon
my mother's mother, Shprintze Thaler, was sitting in the sun
on the steps with the baby on her lap when the two men who
had just robbed the building came out carrying big bags of
stuff—what little they had, my mother always remarked by the
way—and one of them cooed and said "Pretty baby," and the
foolish young mother smiled and thanked him. This of course
was not Grandma Rose's own memory of being that baby, but
a story she had heard about her dead mother, the uneducated,
credulous, fatally compliant Shprintze, a foreigner and a fool
in the big city. From the get-go my mother was determined to
be nobody's fool. If we think back through our mothers, as Virginia Woolf said women do, we also think in reaction to them.

She was Shprintze's fourth baby and only girl, a sturdy child
with broad shoulders, bright hazel eyes, and straight brown
hair. Shprintze herself was "a very nice-looking woman," her
daughter concedes dubiously on the tape; "they were telling
me she was very funny and she was very nice." According to
the family tree drawn by the older of my two cousins Alvin

many years later, my grandmother's hard-to-say name, which sounds like a joke, is a Yiddish corruption of "Esperanza," the mellifluous Spanish word meaning "hope"—evidence, if not quite proof, in Big Alvin's view, that in the late fifteenth century her side of the family had been among the Jews who fled Spain for Eastern Europe. This would suggest some glamorous Sephardic roots that no plain-speaking Thaler ever presumed to claim. Big Alvin's Family Tree also includes a surprisingly artistic ancestor on Shprintze's side, a woodcarver in Alsace.

When my parents in accordance with Jewish custom named me after both my dead grandmothers, "Rochl Shprintze," they Englished the second name as "Sheila," my mother's brother Sam having coined the translation a few years earlier when he named his own daughter Sheila in loving memory of their mother. (Sam the joker always called his girl, heartily, "Shprintz.") Both my parents liked to boast that while trendier friends and relatives had advised them to translate "Rochl" into a romance-novel heroine's name like Rowena, Ramona, or Romola, they had stubbornly stuck to plain "Rachel," unfashionable when I was born. I have always thought that my given name imposed the burden of sobriety on me—making me wonder about poor Shprintze and her squirt or spit of a name.

I never met my grandmother Shprintze, of course, or my patch-proud grandmother Rochl, either. Shprintze died when her daughter was a toddler, a short time after delivering a final blue-eyed boy in the apartment on Broome Street. My mother tells Gabriel that her mother got sick after baby Harry was born, was taken to Mount Sinai Hospital, insisted on going home to tend to her children, but died in the hospital instead. I am surprised to hear this story for the first time: I had always assumed my grandmother had died dramatically at home in childbirth, as a consequence of poor medical care and puerperal fever, like Mary Wollstonecraft. Now this account of her death sounds different to me than it would have done had I heard it earlier: now I hear my mother's pride in there having been an important Jewish hospital in New York, way back then, and I am aware of her awareness that Gabriel himself was born in Mount Sinai Hospital. More painfully, I know that she would choose to die at home and not in a hospital like her mother, and that she hopes Gabriel and I will remember that, and that she is wondering when that will be and where home will be for her then.

That my mother did not remember her mother made her feel shortchanged, to put it in a slangy phrase she liked. When I was growing up, her two closest friends in the apartment house were Mrs. W. and Mrs. K., well-dressed American Jewish matrons whose widowed mothers lived with them and their families. Those little gray-haired women spoke Yiddish fluently as their American daughters flashing bright red nails did only haltingly, and with embarrassment. I remember my mother's admiration of her friends' mothers and her respect for their culinary skills and traditions. She flattered them into teaching her how to cook, as nobody in the busy bakery had ever taken the time to teach her. From them she learned to make dishes from their different parts of Russia, modified for consumption in New York: sweet noodle *kugel* with raisins and pot cheese or cottage cheese and sour cream, for Shavuos; slices of salami—ideally, Isaac Gellis's—fried up with eggs for Sunday night supper; sweet-and-sour stuffed cabbage, both *flaishiks* (with meat) and *pareve* (without milk or meat); and my favorite dish, *kreplach*.

Preparing those pale lumpy dumplings was a brisk morning's work worth watching: my left-handed mother had been "trained" as a child to use her right hand, so, while she wrote and ironed with that one, she cooked ambidextrously. It made her even faster. She would begin the elaborate process of *kreplach*-making by "potting" a piece of *flanken* with garlic, onions, salt and pepper, and a little oil. She usually prepared the dough the next day, pouring flour onto the kitchen table into a little hill, slicing the top off and scooping out a well, then beating her room-temperature eggs into it one by one, diminishing the hill. The soft, rounded mound of dough that resulted sat covered with a clean dish towel while she ground the meat and onions in a squat silvery machine she screwed to the table for that purpose. Then, with a rolling pin on a wooden board, she rolled balls of the sticky dough into flat sheets, sprinkling as needed with flour or water. After cutting the sheets up into squarish pieces, she would place a bit of meat in the center of each, vigorously pinch the dumpling shut between thumb and fingers, and repeat until the flour and the meat mixtures were both simultaneously, magically, gone. The *kreplach* were boiled in water and later served in broth—as a first course. I liked to eat them cold and slightly slimy out of the refrigerator.

My mother loved to cook for the holiday gatherings to which she invited the families of brothers and cousins. She specialized in stuffed things, *kreplach* and roasted chickens and turkeys but also fatty bits of chicken skin or cow intestine (*kishke*) that she filled and sewed up, then roasted alongside the birds. She fussed over the savory filled delicacies she baked in the oven and the sweet ones like *blintzes* that she cooked on top of the stove. She baked *hamantaschen* she stuffed with prunes, not poppyseeds, and long crisp loaves you sliced into to find cocoa, cinnamon, nuts and raisins, and strawberry or apricot jam. Stuffed foods evoked plenty, festivity, coziness, and traditions—home.

From her point of view, a dish was as good as the time and work that went into it: her Friday-night roast chicken was dry, and the lamb chops and liver she broiled for our health even drier. But there were giddy exceptions to the rule of hard work and complexity. One of her favorite party dishes was a dessert served in a big glass bowl, composed of layers of chocolate pudding she managed to sandwich between one or even two of the six delicious flavors of Jell-O—as they recited on the radio, "Strawberry, raspberry, cherry, orange, lemon, and lime." My mother loved Jell-O: it was sweet and translucent and easy to make, and good for you, too. She dismissed as false and un-American the rumors that the main ingredient derived from bones, and she refused to follow the Orthodox crowd and switch to the infelicitously named Ko-Jel, made with a gelatin substitute.

She had learned to cook late, as a married woman, and she was not vain about her cooking. She was delighted, years later, to teach her most interested grandson the right way to make potato latkes for Chanukah, avoiding the food processor and grating the potatoes by hand, then squeezing out their water. But she was not above cutting a corner. In her late seventies she discovered how to rinse and warm and decorate with fresh sliced carrots Manischewitz's gefilte fish from cans, which she mischievously presented to her admiring menfolk at the Passover seder as homemade. My job as *sous chef* was to open and throw out the big cans it came in, and, as she put it, to keep mum, chum. Making gefilte fish from scratch smelled up the house; and she would much rather bake than cook.

When asked for a cake recipe, she would always begin, "You take an egg," then recommend beating into it "as much sugar (or flour) as it takes," in a game in which taking turns into giving. For her it was ordinary to rustle up a batch of *rugelach* together with both chocolate chip and butter cookies, plus two kinds of *mandelbroit*; honey cakes and brownies would often appear on the same day. A birthday sponge cake made with a dozen eggs and garnished with whipped cream and sliced fresh strawberries was on the other hand a major production, the baking process especially shot through with anxiety (will the dough rise? is the inside done?); usually everything was delicious, a great success. Bred in a bakery, she never baked bread—maybe for the same reasons I hardly bake at all.

Possibly—or so I came to think, in Freudian mid-century America—not having had a mother made her, for all her robust self-confidence, unsure of herself in that role. In my middle-aged envy of her adoration of my children and theirs of her, I came to think she had aspired all her life to be not a mother but a grandmother, like the Bubbe Brucha who had so generously and valiantly raised her to be strong and brave and virtuous and always right. Her splendid career as a grandmother was a splashy coda to the unremarkable hard job of mothering, and she reveled in affirming her identity as Grandma Rose. According to my mother, it was my clumsy father, butterfingered and helpless around the house, who had dealt with my first soiled diaper: she hadn't had any idea of what to do with a baby, she explained, having never seen a mother in action. She loved to recall what her friend, my clever Aunt Henia, had said to her in her Russian accent as the two of them contemplated infant me in my crib: "*Raisel: fun dos muz men machen a mensch?*" ("Rose, are you supposed to make a human being out of this thing?")

In the years after World War II, when my brother and I were growing up and our father was working downtown on Sundays and she took us out on adventures by subway—to climb the giant boulders in Central Park, to take the ferry to Staten Island and right back, to a celebratory civic parade—her job, as she saw it, was to get us there and back quickly and safely. She had no interest in exploring the world alongside us, as our father did on our magical early morning walks with him in the country, in the summers, when he would dramatically inhale and praise the fresh country air, and point out beautiful roadside flowers. She hadn't a clue about the finer points of mothering: baffled by the difference between my good behavior in school and my less obedient younger brother's, she marveled all her life at the pungent wisdom of Mr. LeCompte, the principal of P.S. 6 in Astoria, who advised her not to compare her children to one another because (here's the wisdom) every child is different.

She was sentimental and superstitious but not religious. She loved lifting her clear voice to sing the Hebrew prayers and songs at the seder—also the rollicking tragic ballad "The Greene Kuzine," and the "Internationale," and a patriotic Polish anthem with a chorus that went "March, march, Dombrowski." In the car she was likely to belt out, unaccountably, "I'm a rambling wreck from Georgia Tech and a helluvan engineer / A helluva, helluva, helluva, helluva, helluvan engineer." In her old age she mystified her grandchildren by frequently exclaiming "*Guttenyu!*," a Jewish woman's affectionate diminutive for her personal God; she automatically interjected a parenthetical "*Gut zu peeten*," meaning "God should not let it happen," as she knocked on wood when mentioning a misfortune such as—usually—the tragedy of childlessness. She would spit three times, *pu-pu-pu*, to let God know she didn't want what she was about to mention to happen.

But I don't believe she believed in God. At least I'm not sure she did. She clung to tradition as an aspect of the respectability that was all-important to her: a poor motherless child rejected by her father, she needed to be "*balebatish*," a woman of character as her saintly grandmother had raised her to be, a respectable woman, a wife and mother, the lady of the house, a *balebusta*. Muttering a prayer under her breath and covering her eyes with her hands, she lit the Sabbath candles every Friday night; and she kept a strictly kosher home (except for the Jell-O), with separate dishes and pots and pans and silverware for meat and milk and, packed away in newspaper in cardboard boxes stored in the basement, separate sets of dishes and glassware for Passover. I used to think she stuck to the old practices because they were onerous—and/or to please my father. And, like her religious-superstitious foremothers in Eastern Europe, she hoped and prayed for the best by putting eighteen cents in the poor box before one of her children took a test or a journey. The number eighteen is the sum of the two Hebrew letters—counted as numbers from their places in the alphabet—that spell the Hebrew word *chai*, which means "life." Our family's version of a poor box was a battered light-blue tin Jewish National Fund box with a white map of Palestine and later Israel on it, a *pushke* distributed and emptied by Hadassah, the women's Zionist organization of which my mother was a proud member.

No problem, for her, being an American and a Jew at the same time. It was a seamless, not a hyphenated, identity. Over time her view would begin to change: "You're not a Jew, you're an American," she remarked cheerfully, much later, to one of her teenaged grandsons. She herself had always been a Jew (but never a Pole) and now on top of that, in America, she was an American. With my father, she hooted behind their backs at the assimilated Jews whose families had been in America longer, who kept kosher kitchens but ate pork and shrimp when they went to what they (but not my parents) called "the Chinks," or Chinese restaurant, which my parents would never set foot in. Hypocrisy was the moral issue at stake. Why make a *tzimmes* about keeping a kosher home, if you went and ate *trayf* outside the house? Who did you think you were fooling? The targets of their scorn were not only *proste menschen* (literally plain people, but from my parents' point of view also commonplace people) who were stupid and insensitive, but also self-styled *feine menschen*, smug, pleasantly pretentious people like my mother's stiff best friends Mrs. W. and Mrs. K. and their bland and boring mustachioed husbands the doctor and the lawyer, who were having trouble figuring out how to be Jewish and American at once.

The distinction between *proste menschen* and *feine menschen*, a function of taste, education, and sensibility as well as wealth and social class, was more important in my family than the more basic old-world socio-economic distinction between a poor man and a rich one, a *kaptzin* and a *nagid*. Bending the rules of *kashruth*, from my parents' point of view, was a deplorable modern American development: a person should either be kosher or not. "Hypocrites!" they would hoot until we taught them the fashionable Salingeresque variation, "Phonies!" But on the other hand, from my mother's point of view, it was also wrong or silly—*meshuggah*—to be so strictly observant, in America, as for instance to eschew Jell-O, which some people said (but who knew for sure?) was made from the bones of animals. How could such a gruesome thing be true of so clear and pure and sweet a brightly packaged substance? She stuck with Jell-O: once in her late years, when her eyesight was failing, I found in her refrigerator in Florida a whole aspirin accidentally embedded, like a fly in amber, in a small glass bowl of lemon Jell-O she had prepared for herself.

But there were many traditional Jewish customs and ceremonies that defined who she was and could not be tinkered with: lighting the *Shabbes* candles, for example. She (and my father) also lit Yahrzeit candles on the anniversaries of their parents' deaths. To honor the only one of those parents who had died in America, she and her brothers went to the cemetery "to see her." (By the start of the twenty-first century, Acacia Cemetery in Ozone Park, in Queens, was regularly desecrated by vandals every Halloween.) On those excursions, my father would park the car and stay in it with us while she went to the long-dead Shprintze Thaler's grave, where she met up with one or both of her older brothers, Sam and Yussele. My oldest bearded uncle, Chayim, who regularly haunted cemeteries to make his little living as a *shnorrer*, helping those who did not know how to pray for the dead for themselves, would be there too, sometimes, but never my uncle Harry. Harry was impatient with religion until he and his wife joined a grand suburban Jewish congregation on Long Island; he never forgave his parents for abandoning him.

The only likeness I have seen of my maternal grandmother is in a posed studio portrait, bleached and blurry. A slender, angular woman in an old-fashioned shirtwaist and long dark skirt, Shprintze stands, sharp- and hard-faced, severe-looking, among her children in a New York photographer's studio. She leans forward anxiously behind the younger ones, baffled-looking Yussele, who is about five, dressed up in the sailor suit and broad-brimmed hat little boys posed for photographs in then, and the blurry girl baby in a puffy white dress, standing up all by herself, both hands clutching a bunch of flowers. The baby is the brightest, the central figure in the group. The mother and younger children are at a little distance from the dapper father, who is regally seated, as fathers in those photographs were; he and the older boy, Sam, both wear dark suits. Chayim, who would have been about fourteen, is missing from the family portrait, having been left behind safely in Europe as the Bubbe Brucha had insisted. Thirty or so years later, when my mother begged him to send for his daughter from ever-more-dangerous Europe, Chayim refused, on the grounds that the child would be treated like a servant in her aunt's family.

Because this bearded oldest brother of hers was stupid enough to believe that my mother (of all people!) would behave like a wicked stepmother if his daughter, her own niece,

Abraham Isaac Thaler and family, New York (ca. 1907)

came to live with her in America, this older first cousin I never
knew had been murdered in a concentration camp, or, as they
usually said, "the concentration camp"—which makes sense
now that I have learned that Mielec was literally turned into
a work camp and then a death camp by the Nazis, who killed
every Jew they could find in the city. Like many Jews of their
kind, my parents were ingenious in assigning guilt to others
as well as to themselves: subtly, they led me to believe that
had Chayim been smarter and more independent and honest,
had he had a little character and trusted in America and been
less of a hypocrite and more able and willing to Americanize,
I might have lived like a sister with this older girl cousin, and
she might have survived the Nazi slaughter of the European
Jews. Burdened by the responsibilities of an older sister with a

busy mother, haunted by my mother's mournful memory of the daughter she had delivered before me, a beautiful baby born dead at full term, and reminded of that death by the story of my unknown first cousin's terrible early death, I longed throughout my childhood for the sister I should have had.

Before the First World War and Congress's Emergency Quota Act of 1921 there had been no restrictions on European Jews who sought to immigrate to America, and many good reasons for Jews to want to leave Europe. According to the statistics of historians of immigration, Jews were more likely than most immigrants to settle permanently in America. Nevertheless, despite memories of pogroms and poverty, the pull of family and habit and therefore the dream of going back home remained at the back of many people's minds. *"Ich fuhr ahaim"* ("I'm Going Home"), a mournful Yiddish popular song of the interwar years, expresses the yearning to be back in the old country, to live as a Jew among Jews, no longer a stranger in a foreign city. See, for example, I. B. Singer's evocative novel *The Family Moskat*, published in New York in 1950.

My paternal grandfather Avrum Chayim Mayer lived in New York City for forty years, walking to the synagogue to pray two or three times a day, making a meager living as an obscure *melamed*, teaching Hebrew to boys working toward their bar mitzvahs on the Lower East Side and eventually in the South Bronx, where we used to visit him. One room in his apartment was furnished with small desks screwed to the floor to make it a classroom. His father had been a *melamed* before him, in Mielec: one of the many connections between the families of my parents, who met for the first time as adults in New York, is that as a child in Mielec my mother's next older brother Yussele had been a student of my father's grandfather. One of my mother's favorite stories is really her brother Yussele's story, about the Rebbe falling asleep as he chanted the text with the little boys, who mischievously pasted his beard to the table with candle wax that would pull at the beard and wake him painfully when he nodded or lifted his head. The candles, the beard, the chanting, the mischievous boys—it was another world, another time, and you can understand why they wanted to leave, as well as their longing to return to it.

The second wife of my grandfather Avrum Chayim Mayer, who lived with him in the Bronx when I was a child, was also a Galitzianer and a Mielecer. She was named Gittel, Yiddish for "good," which according to my parents she was not. Because her father or perhaps her first husband had been named "Ussher," everyone referred to her as Gittel Ussher's, the two names elided and pronounced Git Lucius. (My mother bitterly recalled that in Mielec she herself had been known to her charitable grandfather's admirers as "Reisel Moishides," as if she were in fact his possession, and not her feckless father's.) Both my parents referred to Git Lucius as The Missus, and called her Missus to her face; my mother addressed my grandfather as Mister. Git Lucius was a bent, mean-spirited woman who served us tasteless cookies that contained neither sugar nor salt.

My mother could never stop telling, always with freshened resentment, the story about the recipe The Missus had given her years before, soon after she got married, which resulted in a cake that ran all over the oven: in a "postal card" that didn't come in the mail until a few days afterward, Git Lucius informed her she had forgotten to mention the baking powder. The mean old lady always wore an orange-blond wig or *shaytel* circled with skinny braids. Unwittingly, she thrilled my brother and me, when our family visited them on Sundays, by hanging her spare wig, set with pin curls, from a post of her bed. A scalp, we were sure, like in the comic books about wild

Indians: my mother liked to tell the story of my American brother shouting out from The Mister and Missus's bedroom in surprise, "Hey, somebody got scalped!" These primitive early Americans seemed foreign to us, and they remained foreigners all their lives in America.

In his forty years in this country, my grandfather Avrum Chayim Mayer never learned to speak or read English. He read the Yiddish newspaper—the right-wing *Morning Journal*, not the socialist *Forverts*.

———————

In 1905, the year my mother was born on Broome Street, the mandarin Anglophile novelist and journalist Henry James detailed his distaste for the jabbering rabble of the Lower East Side of New York in an essay that was later collected in his book *The American Scene*. One wonders how physically close James got to the jabberers: did he hear with his own ears the oddly bastardized English and the foreign diphthongs and gutterals, or did he only see from a distance the wild excess of gestures and shrugs? The hybridizing Yiddish-speaking subculture that James found so abhorrent when he visited New York was to have an extraordinary influence on American culture, American comedy, and the American language. Yiddish tunes and words, and the Jewish style of self-mockery, would flourish for over a century on stages and screens.

Also born on Jewish Broome Street, a few years before my mother, was Molly Picon, the second-generation Galitzianer actress and acrobat who would learn to perfect her Yiddish on her way to becoming a star of Yiddish theater and then film: Molly, as my mother always familiarly referred to her, could still stand on her head in the 1980s, when my mother and I saw her perform live on Broadway. (That same season we also saw Caryl Churchill's *Top Girls*, along with a group of my feminist colleagues delighted to meet my mother.) In *Yiddish Civilisation: The Rise and Fall of a Forgotten Nation* (2005), the British writer Paul Kriwaczek argues for the decisive influence on the American scene of Yiddish speakers from Eastern Europe, who made an outsized mark on not only the theatrical and cinematic culture of twentieth-century America but also American identity. As an example, he points to a Yiddish song my mother used to sing, "The Rebbe Abimelech," which, it turns out, was not the traditional ballad of lamentation it sounds like but a mocking parody of "Old King Cole" written by a couple of talented immigrant jokers in New York and set to a rabbinical-sounding tune. The all-American hamburger, according to Kriwaczek, was invented on the ships that carried Jews from their kosher homes in Europe to America.

Today, there are non-Jews in Maine, Massachusetts, and probably Montana who know and even use words like *maven* and *mazel* and *meshugaas*, *chutzpah* and *shlep* and *shtick*. And language hobbyists of various persuasions disport themselves on the internet inventing amusing Welsh, Japanese, and other mock "pronunciations" of, say, the useful Yiddish word *machetonum*, the meaning of which is illustrated by this engaging sentence: "The parents of our child's spouse are our *machetonum*, and we are theirs."

European Jews came to New York from different countries and cultures. They made *gefilte fish* with or without sugar, and they did or did not add raisins to their different kinds of *kugel*. They sometimes had trouble understanding one another's Yiddish, which commingled German, Hebrew, Slavic, Hungarian, and, increasingly, English words. Henry James was right about the incomprehensible jabber: accents varied, and my mother was occasionally baffled by the recipes of her favorite sister-in-law, her brother Yussele's Russian-born wife.

On the other hand, the Yiddish they shared allowed these people from different nation-states to communicate with one another, all being familiar with the rhythms and inflexions of the *mamaloshen*, a word that means Yiddish, which niftily translates into both "mother tongue" and "women's language." In the *siddurim*, or prayer books, especially designed for women—I have seen one made in America designed to look like a lady's pocketbook, complete with plastic handle—the prayers are in Yiddish rather than Hebrew, which according to some rabbis is a tongue too holy for women's use. Implicit in the Yiddish language is a presumption that the listener will get the speaker's drift—perhaps another reason for the Jamesian distaste. "A language is a dialect with a navy," linguists like to say. There were no navies involved, but among Yiddish speakers there were rigid systems of ranking: the proud Litvak, for example my mother-in-law, believed that her vowels proved her social superiority to her Galitzianer *machetaynista*.

The Yiddish language changed as the Jews moved through Europe, picking up one word here and another there, fashioning multilingual proverbs. The *mamaloshen*—the mother tongue but also the Word of the Mother, as a post-Lacanian feminist might put it—had many fathers. From even a casual acquaintance with Yiddish, it's clear that this language—we're not talking about the Bible, here—cannot be the work of a single Author.

Jews (as well as *goyim*) have had different attitudes toward a language that was rooted in their culture's difference, and intensified their difference from others. For some, Yiddish was the language of home and intimacy: it seemed to others the more distasteful for that very reason. Jews who imagine themselves to be better than other Jews tend to boast of their ignorance of Yiddish: German Jews, French Jews, Italian and British Jews—even some who are only a generation removed from a *shtetl*—often falsely claim to have no knowledge of that embarrassingly humble, not-euphonious, inelegant language (compare, e.g., pride in one's native French). My mother-in-law, for instance, the daughter of an immigrant Litvak junk dealer, was born in Buffalo, New York, graduated from high school there, and aspired to gentility. Delicately, as if she did not quite own the word, she would call a non-Jewish young woman a *shiksie* instead of a *shiksa*, which made my mother laugh at her—and reminded me that my mother herself had taught us to call the sweet bread Jews call *challah* "*challie*," with all-American vowels, when we were children.

Jews who know only a little Yiddish have popularized harshly negative words like *shmuck*, *shlang*, *shtunk*, and *shlemiel*—sneering, jeering words with a bad odor that have been welcomed into the vernacular as if non-Jews really needed them. The best example of the way many children of immigrants think about the taint of Yiddish and its alleged authenticity is the joke about the man with the thick Jewish accent who successfully auditions for the starring role of Hamlet, and then accounts for his wonderfully plummy rendering of a familiar soliloquy by saying, with a shrug, "*Vell, det's ecting.*" The joke is that low Jews who ape high gentiles are only acting roles, and that Yiddish itself is an ugly, whiney language—the vulgate, as opposed not only to Hebrew, the sacred language, but to grammatical language generally.

One scholar has argued persuasively that the 1910 census of Galicia inaccurately reflects the proportion of German to Polish speakers because the survey didn't offer "Yiddish" as a choice—presumably because it wasn't considered a proper language. The early Zionists were scornful of Yiddish and/or dubious about its credentials: around the turn of the nineteenth century, they successfully revived the "dead" language of Hebrew, which has sustained an astonishing return to life in

Israel. But meanwhile many brilliant journalists, playwrights, and novelists of the late nineteenth and early twentieth centuries just as successfully installed Yiddish among the literary languages.

Some American-born Jews my age, born either to religious Jews or to Jews from left-leaning backgrounds, were taught to read and write Yiddish as children as a matter of national pride: not a few of them, although born and raised in America, learned English as a second language in school. In contrast, my bearded, Orthodox, right-wing, anti-Zionist grandfather Avrum Chayim Mayer agreed with my parents' view that Yiddish was irrelevant to the life of an educated American girl or boy. "Why are you reading that garbage about those silly people, Danny?" my historian son recalls my mother asking him when she found him with a copy of *A Bintel Brief*, the collection of letters to and from the editor of the *Forverts*, translated into English, which he valued as a source of information about the lives of Jewish immigrants to New York. She considered herself too American to read or value the *Forverts*. When my grandfather came to visit us in the bungalow colony, in the summer, minus Git Lucius but bringing with him his own two sets of glatt-kosher pots for my mother to cook his super-kosher food in, he spoke to me in Yiddish and I replied in English. We understood one another pretty well.

My parents spoke Yiddish with him, as they did with one another: I learned to understand the secret language because I wanted to know what they were saying about us children (what else did they have to talk about?). My grandfather was both entertained and pleased by my sketchy comprehension of his language. We had a little joke about it. There was a town near Mielec called Tuna that he was reminded of by my favorite lunchtime sandwich, and with a twinkle he would say to me, *"Nu, Rachel, noch a mal fish fun Tuna?"* ("You're eating fish from Tuna again?") He called me Rachel with a throaty "r," never the Yiddish Rochl. I was his only granddaughter.

At one point in my early fifties, when I was two weeks into a research trip to Paris and at the tipping point of thinking and dreaming in French, I was strolling on a lovely spring evening across the beautiful colonnaded Place des Vosges, in the heart of the aristocratic district of the Marais, when I was astonished to find myself understanding what the family walking behind me were saying to one another. Something ordinary about a blue dress and matching shoes to be worn to a wedding. I was aware that their language was neither English nor French for a long moment before I recognized that they were speaking Yiddish. Like the Lower East Side of New York, the Marais is an old Jewish neighborhood.

If the unconscious is structured like a language, as French theory had it in the 1980s, that language would be Yiddish. Or perhaps it's only that Yiddish speakers are sometimes only half-aware of falling into that language. My younger friend E. tells the story of her grandmother, a woman of my mother's generation, who was the chairperson of the English department in a New York public high school in the 1950s. One day, after visiting a colleague's classroom to give him instructions about a department-wide exam, she realized only after she had left the room that she and the teacher had been conversing in Yiddish, so as to prevent the students—the children—from understanding them.

Even now, after I have tried to channel my parents by learning to read and write Yiddish, hearing or overhearing its particular music, as I did on the Place des Vosges that evening long ago, gives me a comfortable sense of secret comprehension even when I don't quite follow: listening to someone speak that language is like being borne along on an unexpected wave of music to the place where I learned it as a spy listening in on my parents. Even when I don't know most of the words, I seem to get the drift.

———————

My mother's birth in Manhattan was recorded in the appropriate civic bureau as Reisel Feige, later informally translated into Rose Florence, or, variously, Rose Faith. She pretty much dropped the middle name, as much later I would drop the Sheila from my own name—as a useless vestigial trait like an appendix. Sometimes she liked to imagine herself as an exotic Rosa, like Rosa Luxemburg, perhaps. Photos of her in the 1920s suggest she might have modeled herself—pouting red lips, penciled eyebrows, bobbed hair—on her contemporary Rosa Ponselle, famously the first American star of the Metropolitan Opera.

She delighted her grandsons, decades later, by telling them she had been "a flepper," and she had photos of herself in snappy asymmetrical hats and flounced dresses to prove it. Her friends and neighbors and her American sisters-in-law knew her as Rose and occasionally Rosie. Her favorite sister-in-law Henia called her Raisel in her Russian accent, and she sometimes affectionately called Henia Genia, a pronunciation suggested by one romanization of the Cyrillic spelling. In old age she liked being called "Grandma Rose" by her children's friends as well as her treasured grandchildren; but she knew herself and addressed herself as Reisel, as her family and my father knew her, the diminutive packed into the name.

Short but not small, Reisel had regular features: hazel eyes, a straight nose, and straight brown hair she liked to wear long, rolled, and pinned up in what they called pompadours when I was a child. She was vain about her good looks and good taste.

In old age she raged against the falling out of her hair, refusing to cut it short as I suggested, being still fearful, long after my father's death, of a bad haircut that would make her look like his customer, Mrs. Meridi, whom he had once mockingly suggested she resembled. But she liked to talk about an early landlady's little girl, in New York, who had demanded to be given "a Rosie bob," an independent woman's short haircut like hers: for a milliner especially, it makes sense for one's hair to be a node of vanity. There was a streak of gray in the upsweep she affected in the 1940s, and it broadened as I grew. In her early fifties, her hair was all white like her handsome brother Harry's. She disdained to dye it: wouldn't think of such flagrant inauthenticity!

Small of bosom and booty, she had a big belly and no waist at all: her long brassiere hooked onto the top of the boned, flesh-colored girdle she always wore under her clothes, encasing her. Reisel was, as she knew, attractive despite that belly— or because of it. Still mentally *zaftig* on her deathbed, my poor scrawny mother murmured with satisfaction, upon being introduced to her third grandson's fiancée, "He got the best one!"—meaning that this pretty girl had more flesh on her than the other two. She knew she was charming and personally charismatic: she liked men of all ages and loved to boast about the "colored" piano mover whose sweaty back she scratched, at his request, while he held up the piano. "Lady, would you please scratch my back?" she imitated him, then shrugged. "So I did."

But she never thought of, as she boasted, any man but my father. This in contrast to her dainty sister-in-law Henia: whenever she got the chance, my mother recalled that Henia, whom she herself had introduced to her amiable brother Yussele, had been overly friendly with the purser on the ship to Europe on her honeymoon, and later on with the dentist and the pharmacist, in addition to god knows who else—and that when he heard rumors, her husband, my poor uncle Joe who worked in a dairy shop, had slept on the couch for two weeks, as my more manly father would never have done. My parents were not physically or verbally demonstrative with one another—or with us. But when they came home, all dressed up and glossy from a wedding or bar mitzvah or similar "affair," she wearing her gold jewel-encrusted "cocktail" watch that had a little hinged door covering the dial, my father invariably reported to us that she'd been the most beautiful woman there. She didn't disagree with him.

But sometimes she would dismiss his comment and sardonically quote—of all people!—The Missus: *"Ins ze'mir shenner,"* "To us, we are better-looking." Like the jolly popular Yiddish song *"Bei mir bist du shane,"* which translates as "To me you are pretty," the phrase undercuts the compliment it pays. Irony.

---

The past is indeed a foreign country. It is hard for me to understand how Ahzhe Thaler could do what he did after his wife died—leave an infant in an orphanage in America, leave his tiny daughter with his parents—but it is also hard to figure out what else he could have done. Probably his friends and relatives agreed that the right thing to do was deposit his infant son in the Hebrew Home in New York and take his two little boys and the littler girl back home. A relation of Shprintze's who was living then in New York, a brother or maybe even her own mother, the baby's grandmother, allegedly meant to adopt the child, but the one night he stayed with them he wet the bed, and so they returned him to the orphanage. Hard to know how old he would have been when they expected him not to wet the bed. Was the harsh truth, which was that nobody wanted the infant, buried or forgotten because they, or because she, became ashamed of it over time, or was it a secret from the start? Did anyone ever know the truth? What would have been the right thing to do?

In her eighties, my mother's voice would rise incredulously, in outrage, when she talked about her father: "Did you ever hear such a thing, a man comes back from America and dumps three children with his mother and goes off after women? He wasn't a nice man; my mother's family didn't like him; he wasn't nice to my mother. Harry he left in America as a baby, when she died; Yussele and Sam and I he dumped with his mother; Miriam he divorced because he met Paircha. She had a store that her husband left her, and he liked her." My mother never stopped being embarrassed by her long-dead father's sexuality, so different from the purity of her pious grandfather.

In her one written account of the story of her life, my mother lies outright, claiming that Ahzhe left the baby behind with her mother's relatives in New York. When I was a little girl, she told me that nice ladies on the ship had helped her father take care of her on his way back with her across the ocean. It was embarrassing even to consider the problem: how could a man take care of a little girl? Modesty and propriety as well as a man's innate ineptness forbade it.

There are many things I don't know about my mother's family, especially concerning the character of my grandfather Ahzhe Thaler—for example, his politics, if he had them. Not learned in the Bible like his father (or mine), he was a modern man—a secular man—but it's unclear what that meant, in his time, to him. Living in New York in 1903–1907 or so, how aware was he of European politics, and specifically of Russian and Polish politics? What was he thinking about his children's futures when he dumped his daughter on his mother around 1907–1908? Did he think that a part of Poland near Russia, where there were pogroms, was a safer place for a Jew than New York? Had he originally intended to immigrate to America, and been thwarted only by the accident of his wife's death? How disappointed had he been in his own life, toward the end of it? In 1917, after the war, when he requested an American passport for himself, the authorities wrote back that to qualify for such a document he was obliged to present proof that he had intended to become an American citizen all those years ago. He seems not to have done that. But what in fact had his intentions been?

It is a Jewish man's obligation to marry. I remember my uncle Chayim many years later in New York, after his wife and daughter had been murdered by the Nazis, phoning one eligible widow after another from my parents' apartment, desperate to find a woman to take care of his laundry and meals. "Hallo, Mrs. Zilberstein? Chayim Thaler here." And very soon after that hanging up the phone, then hanging his head, disappointed by having been turned down.

Dapper Ahzhe Thaler with his blue eyes and golden beard was more attractive than his awkward, bumbling oldest son would turn out to be. He had better luck with women: he was married or almost married to a second wife, Miriam, before he encountered the formidable Paircha, who would become the mother of his second daughter. It was universally acknowledged in his culture that a widower, especially one with small children, must find himself a wife. In her interview with Gabriel, my mother says grudgingly in his defense that Ahzhe after all had been a young man, then—clear code for a sexually active man. My uncle Harry, who had been left in his infancy in the New York orphanage, all his life bitterly referred to the father he never knew as "the old whoremaster."

Paircha, the round-shouldered widow with two young daughters whom Ahzhe married after returning to Mielec, set him up at the counter of a fancy food store that sold the Levantine sweetmeats imported from Istanbul to Lviv that were loved by Ashkenazi Jews: candy-coated Jordan almonds and roasted and salted almonds and cashews and pistachio nuts; sweet dried raisins, plums, and apricots; halvah; and the Lindt chocolate from Switzerland that my mother all her life was sure was the very best—a certainty she passed on to me. She recalled sexy scenes of Ahzhe cracking open a walnut, dipping the meat in red wine, and delicately placing it on his new wife's tongue. Covertly, so his wife couldn't see, Ahzhe thrust sweets into little Reisel's hand when she visited her father's store. I imagine Paircha watching him as she watched the merchandise, sitting behind the cash register, wearing a black dress and a little gold chain around her neck like a gimlet-eyed shopkeeper's wife in a novel by Balzac. She was a woman to reckon with: according to my cousin, her granddaughter, scrappy Paircha spent a night in jail once, for selling cigarettes—which only soldiers had a right to sell. My mother never got over resenting her.

Ahzhe dutifully invited Reisel, at one point, to move from her grandmother's house and live with his new family, but he didn't seem enthusiastic. And at ten or twelve she was not eager to embrace a sexy new stepmother. She wasn't eager, either, to leave her grandmother and the noisy extended family living above the sweet-smelling bakery, where she was the leader of a band of admiring boy cousins. Another little cousin, named Deborah but always called Dullah, was born into the bakery family in 1914; in September 1918, Ahzhe's new wife Paircha gave birth to her baby girl, my cousin Adrianne's mother Ruth or Roozha, a force of nature who would become a popular yoga teacher in Washington, DC, where she lived in the Watergate Building right next door to John and Martha Mitchell, who were important figures in the Nixon administration.

My mother, as a teenager, didn't like Paircha or Paircha's daughters or certainly Paircha's and Ahzhe's new baby, whom she was put in charge of as she was of little Dullah at the bakery. She preferred running around with her boy cousins to mothering baby dolls and baby girls. The one night she had spent at her father's house she fell out of bed, cutting her forehead deeply and leaving a permanent scar. She came back to live out her happy, hardworking childhood as the cherished child of the Bubbe Brucha, who didn't want her to leave home—"Say I had a child late in life," she quoted the generous Bubbe as saying. Until she was eighteen, she slept in one bed with Brucha, the surrogate mother whose swollen legs and feet she was awakened to rub in the middle of the night, and whom she invoked at the head of a proverb every day of her life with a prefatory "As my grandmother used to say."

An enlarged bluish-gray colorized version of a photograph that Brucha had been forced to have taken for a passport so she could cross a new national border to visit a sick daughter—the only kind of urgency that could persuade her to break the religious injunction against graven images—hung in my parents' living room when I was a child. Later it dominated their living room in Florida. The stoical sitter is grim-faced, wearing a kerchief or babushka knotted under her chin; a piece of dark silk above her lined forehead covers the shaved head beneath. I was glad to let my brother take the picture home with him after my mother died. The piercing light eyes had always terrified me. As a child I used to imagine the Bubbe Brucha's stern spirit descending in the dust motes to judge me severely: my mother always described her as a perfectly just and fair woman, who was called in to resolve disputes by warring families, as well as to lay hands on a dangerously sick neighbor. I always knew I fell short of her high standard of perfection.

But judging the characters of one's children and grandchildren is not a real human problem: one tends to be blind or forgiving or dead. The serious problem is judging one's parents or grandparents: that is, how not to? For years I shared my mother's and my youngest uncle's bitter points of view and imagined Ahzhe, who dumped them, as a weakling and a quitter, a spoiled mama's boy who didn't even try to take care of his own children. But now I think about it this way: what else, in his world, could a poor man brought up to believe in a set of constraints and prohibitions related to sex and the body—a man, furthermore, with such a kind and capable mother— have done? Raise a little girl himself?

Over the years, watching my own children grow and change, I have wondered about the effect on his motherless children of Ahzhe Thaler's dramatic dereliction of paternal duty. My handsome uncle Harry, the baby he abandoned to the Hebrew Home in New York, turned out to be the most successful of Ahzhe's four sons—was, indeed, his only successful son, eventually a partner in a Wall Street firm, rich and happily married, with a loving daughter he doted on. And now it seems to me that Ahzhe's uncertain moves toward and away from America overdetermined his daughter Reisel's character, her politics of generosity, her hatred of dogma and parochialism, her cultural pluralism—not only her commitment to the rights of the underdog but also her daft notion that, for instance, Queen Elizabeth of England, photographed in a babushka by Hermes or Harrod's, was "really just a nice, plain woman, like one of my aunts."

———————

Ahzhe Thaler, born in Mielec in 1870, would not have believed you, had you managed to inform him that only ten years after his death not only his Americanized sons but also his discarded daughter Reisel would be voting for an American president, the Nineteenth Amendment having been ratified in 1920, four years before her return to New York. Or that at least one of his children was savoring the jaunty lyrics of "Wintergreen for President," a choral number in George and Ira Gershwin's *Of Thee I Sing* (1931), a musical-comedy send-up of American electioneering: "He's the man the people choose! / Loves the Irish and the Jews!"

The position of Jews in New York City and in America more generally was changing dramatically, offstage as well as on, in the between-wars period when my mother was turning herself into a real American, a patriot and a citizen. In the late 1920s and early 1930s, when Al Smith was governor of New York and she started stepping out on the town with my father—that is, when she talked him into stepping out with her—*Abie's Irish Rose* was one of the biggest hits on Broadway. It became Broadway's longest-running play: see, for example, Lorenz Hart's casually ironic lyrics to "Manhattan" (1926): "Our future babies / We'll take to *Abie's / Irish Rose* / We hope they live to see / It close." The theme of immigration was successful on Broadway long before Lin-Manuel Miranda's *Hamilton* (2015) reprised the Whitmanesque subject: in the 1920s and 1930s, with a hint of a Yiddish accent, then, American immigrant culture celebrated itself.

That she arrived in Manhattan on March 17, 1924, St. Patrick's Day, came to seem to Reisel Thaler, aka Rose Mayer, increasingly significant over time, as in her time lucky immigrants like her were changing the character of America.

# CHAPTER 3

# MIELEC

Mielec, town in Rzeszow Province, S.E. [formerly Galicia]. The Jewish community of Mielec was first organized in the middle of the 17th century. [In the early 20th century,] the Jewish population . . . remained relatively static, increasing from 2,766 (56% of the total population in 1880) to 2,819 (57%) in 1900 and 3,280 (53%) in 1920, then falling to 2,807 (50%) in 1920. . . . By September 1929, the population had reached 4,000. On Sept. 13, 1939, the eve of Rosh Ha-Shanah, the Germans set a synagogue aflame and pushed 20 persons into the burning building. . . . Mielec was among the first cities that the German Government made *Judenrein*. Near the workshops of the Heinkel Airplane Company Mielec had a labor camp under the direct auspices of the S.S. . . . The mortality rate at the camp reached more than 15 per day, excluding the sick who were shot.

MUSEUM OF THE JEWISH DIASPORA, Israel, 1992

Mielec, Poland, today is a city with a population of 65,000 people, none of them known to be Jewish.

ROCHELLE G. SAIDEL, *Mielec, Poland: The Shtetl That Became a Nazi Concentration Camp* (2012), p. 1

[The] characterization of Eastern Europe as the intermediary domain between Europe and Asia, between civilization and barbarism, was as old as the Enlightenment.

LARRY WOLFF, *The Idea of Galicia: History and Fantasy in Habsburg Political Culture* (2010), p. 243

"Mellitz," my parents pronounced it, leaving out the "y" sound and accenting the mellowed first syllable. When I first saw the Polish name printed out on a map, their mispronuncia-

tion seemed to me yet another mark of their Galitzianer limitations, their crude inattention to linguistic detail a sign of
their embarrassing awkwardness in modern Western culture.
In fact, as I have learned, the name of the place in Yiddish is
"Mellitz," and as I read more I begin to understand that various pronunciations were tolerated and understood in Galicia,
where speakers of Polish and German lived—matter-of-factly,
if often uncomfortably—among speakers of Russian and Ro-
manian and Yiddish.

When my brother and I were children, Mielec wasn't a place
you could tell people your family came from and expect them
to recognize it, like Sicily or Dublin or Warsaw or Berlin. No
one outside the family seemed to have heard of it—and yet for
years strange people kept turning up in our kitchen, winter
evenings, to tell my parents terrible stories about what had
happened there. I never had a mental image of the place. To
me, Mielec was a vague, gray, grim antithesis of our world, an
alternative universe. It was shapeless like a monster in a bad
dream—that is, it kept assuming different shapes.

It was hard even to say what country it was in, Austria or
Hungary or Poland, as it also changed places, probably because
nobody wanted it. It was "a small town," my mother used to begin deprecatingly, "a very small town," by which I understood
that it was narrow-minded, not cosmopolitan; but sometimes
she would insist it was in fact a city. Literally and metaphorically, it was muddy and cold, dark and primitive, and in some
unspeakable way as terrible as death—a dead-end place, for
sure. Also full of dead people related to us. It was also, fortu-
nately, far away and long ago, as if it had never been. No one
could go back to it even if they wanted to, and who would want
to? Riddled with superstition and misery, it was all gone now,
as impossible to visit as a place in a fairy tale or a scary movie.
Which was okay by our mother, it seemed—even though she

sometimes seemed nostalgic for the land of her youth—and certainly okay by us.

Today, of course, a curious child can see the outline of the city's history on the internet. There are photographs of monuments and nature walks and hotels in and around Mielec. You can even find a photo of an old postcard that was printed, incredibly, in the 1930s to lure tourists to visit the place. There are photographs of airplanes that were made in the German factory there (some with legible, recognizable brand names), and pictures of people in old-fashioned clothing, and of horse-drawn carts and now-extinct automobiles on the streets around the marketplace. The Rynek—marketplace—of my mother's memories turns out to have been a large empty square surrounded by two-story stone houses festooned with simple shop signs: in the early 1940s, Nazi soldiers assembled Jews they had rounded up on that square before murdering them.

It is no problem to find on the internet the two images that telegraph the terrible story of the city in the twentieth century. The first is a photograph of the big stone synagogue with two Moorish towers that was taken at some time before September 1939, when the Germans burned the building along with the Jews praying inside it. The second photograph is of the ruin sinking back into the earth. The "before" picture shows tiny black-garbed men standing in front of the building, with a small group of women at the side: Jewish congregants. In the sunny, overexposed "after" photo, blond boys play in the dirty ruins.

Six months or so before she died, I was astonished to hear my mother recite the names of the shops around the city square to another old woman she had just met, who had told her that she too was from Mielec. My mother had met the woman, who seemed confused and barely understood her detailed recital, in the Jewish nursing home near my apartment in Manhattan.

They both were residents there, and my mother was showing off her mental acuity to the stranger—and to me.

The nursing home was the place where, another day, as I pushed her in a wheelchair down a corridor, a tall, well-dressed fiftyish lady in full makeup stopped us and looked down at her with incredulity and said, "Mrs. Mayer? Is that really you?" Clearly neither an inmate of the institution nor a visitor, the younger woman was evidently noticing and recognizing my mother for the first time.

"Oh, hello, Sharon," my mother replied heartily, without missing a beat, not at all surprised to see her. The woman, it turned out, was the director of the institution. "I'm fine, and how are you, and how is your brother Howie?"

"Howard is fine, doing very well, thanks, he's a dentist now with three children," Sharon replied, then hesitated for a minute. "And how is Alan?"

I frantically rummaged through my memory, but still had no idea who this old friend of my family might be. When my mother and I got back to her room, she explained that Sharon was a girl in the neighborhood who had been sweet on my brother Alan, who had been her brother Howie's friend, years ago. We're talking thirty, forty years.

Memories vary. My mother's memory was better than most, better than mine. But she didn't recall everything she could remember.

---

My parents situated anything that had been done or said in Mielec "*in die haim*" or "back home"—in my father's strongly Germanic pronunciation, "*heim*." It had been home for them both, as it probably had been for most of their ancestors for over two hundred years: had they met and married there rather than in New York City, it would have been, incredibly, home for my brother and me as well, and we would not have spoken English, not have been Americans, not have been in any way ourselves. Fact is, born when we were in the late 1930s, we probably would not have been at all: we would have been murdered as babies, sadistically roasted on the point of a bayonet or casually tossed into a burning building, as in the movies, or strangled or smothered or kicked to death, or killed in the gas chambers as our first cousin, our uncle Chayim's daughter, had been, along with many second and third cousins we would never know of. I imagined it.

In her old age my mother would sometimes have a sudden memory of Mielec, the weirdness of the place and its radical difference from the way we live now. Few physical details of her hometown emerged from the stories she told us, which were always about people, feelings, ethics. After I wrote down the following rambling after-dinner musings of hers, I tried to imagine a section of a city with high wooden sidewalks and strangely empty streets:

You know they say George Burns has writers, but I know he writes his own material. All the jokes are his. He's like his grandfather—I knew his grandfather in Europe. He was a very clever man. In Europe, he used to go to weddings, and tell stories and have sayings—he would get up and talk. Very bright. A very religious man, with a beard down to here. I remember one day, I was playing outside with my friend, and we saw him coming to visit my grandfather. I was afraid of him—he was a very angry man, such an angry man, and with a big stick. And he was coming to the sidewalk—but sidewalks weren't like they are here, there was a big step up, high—and he was a very old man, little and frail, and he tried to get up the step, and tried again, and he was almost falling, and he finally got up. I went and I took him by the arm and I helped him up. And he said to my grandfather later that I was right to do that even though a girl was forbidden to touch a man, that I wasn't like the Jew in the old story who saw a woman drowning and let her drown because it was forbidden for a man to touch a woman.

Even as a girl she was proud of honoring the spirit, rather than the letter, of the Jewish laws about how to behave to other people. As Jews—as all good people—should do and did, then and now.

———————

In my childhood, Mielec usually came up in conversation in pointed contrast to the luxury and privilege our little family enjoyed in a three-room apartment on the ground floor of a red-brick apartment house on the corner of Twenty-Eighth Avenue and Thirty-Sixth Street in Astoria, Queens, a short ride by subway and ferry to the Statue of Liberty in bountiful, enlightened America. The statue that had the poem by the Jewish woman poet Emma Lazarus engraved on a plaque on the base beneath it, "Give me your tired, your poor, / Your huddled masses yearning to breathe free." In America we were not tired or poor or yearning. God bless America, as Irving, originally Israel, Berlin had taught the whole great country to sing. I was a year and a half old in November 1938, when Kate Smith first sang "God Bless America" on the radio. For the rest of her life my mother admired Kate Smith, not only her voice and her message but also Kate herself for being, like her, a big girl and proud of it. In America, lucky children like us had all the food we wanted, and nourishing food, too, made by our loving mother's own hands; we went to cool off in the Catskill Mountains,

summers, and had nothing to do but go to school and play—
and go to Hebrew school, and take piano lessons, in my case.

In Mielec, the food was meager as well as tasteless, and none
of it was good for you. There was not even a rumor of the broiled
lamb chops and baked Idaho potatoes my mother regularly put
on our plates along with canned peas and carrots. And often
there wasn't enough food. "If the soup had a little piece of meat
in it, my grandfather got it, on a spoon," my mother recalled
in equivocal tones: she didn't like it, but that was how it had
to be there, even if it was unfair. And Moishidle, her grandfather, was old and skinny and needed nourishment. The Jews
of Mielec were poor—yes, her grandmother was very friendly
with some nice *goyim*, and a *Shabbes goy* came in to tend the
fire on Friday night, but of the people in my mother's stories,
except for the rare philosophical Polish woodcutter or farmer
whom the broadminded Bubbe Brucha had democratically befriended, the named characters were all Jews. If a young girl
was late getting home, as a child, and Jews were being beaten
up by the antisemites that day, in Mielec, her grandmother
didn't worry, even though they had no telephone, because she
knew that another lady—of course a Jewish lady—would take
the child in.

If you were a girl in Mielec, you worked hard in the house
and in the bakery, scrubbing and scouring, and you helped
with the younger children—whereas lucky American children like us didn't do any work at all. At one point in history
the state law mandated that all children in Mielec—even Jewish girls—had to go to school, and there were truant officers
who enforced that law, but my mother claimed never to have
moved up beyond fifth grade. She vividly remembered her
life before the First World War, before she was eight or nine:
she carried huge sacks of flour, and in winter she hauled those
sacks as well as barrels of water to the bakery by sled, with one

or another of the four motherly aunts she lived with running behind to help keep the burden upright. Her pale eyes flashed with energy when she talked about that, and I could almost see the little girl inside her—or maybe a slightly older girl of eleven or twelve—recalling the past. Her view of her childhood brightened somewhat as my childhood ended and she grew older and more nostalgic: on reflection it seemed to her that her family had not been so poor after all. "My grandmother had a big house," she would recall in her lonely old age. "There were a lot of people there."

In the black-and-white snapshots my husband took on his trip to Eastern Europe in 1977, the building that had housed the Bubbe Brucha's bakery and the family's home upstairs is a simple low rectangular structure like a small factory in Queens. But in my mind, in my childhood, Mielec was a mythic place, not so much a particular place as a lost way of life, or an era from a folktale. I was startled to glimpse and recognize it—as it nearly seemed—only once, in 1959, when I woke up suddenly from a deep sleep in a train that had taken me from Italy to Yugoslavia, and saw outside the window, in the early morning mist, a group of sturdy women in babushkas, silent and unsmiling, plying shovels on the railroad tracks. I recognized them as the background characters in my mother's stories, her grandmother's neighbors, or their ghosts: the grim impoverished *goyim* of Eastern Europe.

Maybe we inherit our parents' memories as well as their genes. "Close your eyes and think of Paris," my father would say to soothe me when I couldn't fall asleep as a child, and I would entertain a vision of the City of Light—I had seen glamorous photographs—where he had once been unimaginably free and happy, before he came to America and settled down. Apparently, I also had in my head a very different bleak vision of Eastern Europe, derived from my parents' ambivalent memories of muddy Mielec, which my mother, to remember it, passed on to us.

———————

At our parents' insistence, my two-years-younger brother and I were obliged to be smart in school: they made it clear that, quite literally, their lives depended on our academic success. Later, when we were adolescents, they made it equally clear that they would kill themselves if one of us God forbid married a non-Jew—as my brother did a few years after my father died at eighty. My mother loved the bride, who had been poor like her, growing up.

Early on I realized that being good at school did not make us popular with our envious aunts and uncles and cousins, or with the neighbors. More or less involuntarily, and certainly without acknowledging it, our parents taught us to be *choizik machers*, people who make fun of other people for being, well, not so smart. Like Jane Austen's Mr. Bennet, we lived to laugh at the neighbors—and I suppose to try to tolerate being laughed at in our turn, should the neighbors have the wit to laugh back. Which of course most of them did not.

Kinds of stupidity are carefully distinguished from one another, in Yiddish: one man might be just a harmless *naar* or fool, while his more offensive brother was a *proste Yid* or *am Haaretz*, a simple and stupidly simpleminded earthy Jew. While being smart sometimes seemed to be a Jewish trait, there were more than enough dumb Jews around to provide entertainment. One of my father's favorite jokes was about the Jew who admits that Yes, certainly he could be a little richer, a little healthier, and maybe even a little taller—but smart? He was as smart as anyone else.

My father was smarter. My mother's cousin Dave the Greenpoint greengrocer addressed him as "Professor." My father read old books in multiple volumes and talked sweepingly about politics and economics and history; he brought us up to worship language and revere writers, and libraries, and schools, and scholarship and of course scholarships to pay the tuition, which we duly earned. Obligingly and for the fun of pleasing him, we impressed our teachers in school and in Hebrew school, which we went to two or three times a week, after school, as some of our friends in Astoria went to their Catholic or Armenian or Ukrainian religious schools on Wednesday afternoons.

Like the children of new Americans before and after us, we were urged to excel, to get good grades ("marks") that would make us admired and ensure our prosperity in later life. Although comedians and social scientists have simplified the truth, success—a combination of wealth, respectability, and social status—was imagined in different ways in different Jewish families in America after World War II. A lot of postwar comedy mocked the immigrant Jewish aspiration to assimilation and riches: the sons who aimed to be professional men, ideally doctors but if not that lawyers, or at least dentists, or accountants, or pharmacists at the very least, or real-estate men, those aristocrats of salesmen. The daughters would be the proud wives of professional men, maybe after teaching a little in the beginning, or filling in as a part-time bookkeeper in a brother's or a husband's business. Our family was a little different: my father insisted that Mrs. W.'s husband the doctor, a specialist in urology, was basically just a plumber. What he wanted my brother to be was a genius.

Raised to value learning (the Torah, Truth) over mere worldly wealth, and to keep his hands soft and clean, my father himself had been very good at school from the beginning, sitting under the table at the *cheder* at three, secretly learn-

ing more than the older boys. He and my mother with him
aimed higher than their neighbors, and more obliquely. Their
children were to be readers who knew what they were talking
about, real professors at esteemed universities, people of culture superior to ordinary *"proste menschen"* (literally "simple
people," but as my father contemptuously spat the words out,
stupid and vulgar and ignorant as well). In an era that honored
Einstein and Oppenheimer and even the minor scientists who
helped us compete with the Russians, my blond, blue-eyed,
and brilliant brother would be a physicist or a mathematician,
working at higher mathematics for the government at an esteemed university like Columbia or Princeton, where he did
in fact earn degrees. Many years later, my brother ruefully
reflected to me that our father would turn over in his grave if
he knew his son would end up teaching at the Jewish Brandeis
University and his daughter at also pretty Jewish Brooklyn
College. As my mother always said, our father was a snob. In
her view this was only reasonable.

My mother's two best friends and the small-time professional men they had married were tolerated with difficulty
by my father as nice enough dummies who had nothing to say
about politics, or indeed anything that was written about in
the *New York Times*. He didn't pretend to have much in common with them. Neither did he hide his preference for a long
talky evening with his eccentric cousins, bachelor brothers
and self-taught furriers with whom he would chew over the
tragedies of European history. But in the days when we were
growing up in middle-class Astoria, it was so important for my
mother to be "normal," and she was so energized by the role
that he indulged her—and tried out his own new role as The
Average Man. A Tolerant Man with a scholarly historian's perspective. This was years before he got old and frankly cranky
and we wickedly, behind his back, called him by the name for

Turkey that we had learned in school: The Sick Man of Europe. As The Average Man, he voiced middle-of-the-road political views. He tolerated his wife's friends and their husbands as nice people to play canasta with once a week, pleasant Americans, but *proste menschen*, as my father would say, *au fond*. Simple people. Sometimes he summed them up kindly and condescendingly as "naïve."

Unlike these Jews raised in America, my parents spoke to one another in Yiddish. They did not pride themselves on being bilingual, as French- or German-speaking immigrants did, and to us they seemed to be speaking not quite another language but a Jewish kind of English, English with a heavy accent. They slid from one language to the other in a single sentence, as in "What about a *bissel* chicken soup with a *shtick broit*?" (a little chicken soup with a piece of bread). Theirs was not so much a different language as a different way of talking, as *Franglais* or *Spanglish* is for some people, a lax unlettered out-of-school argot: Yinglish or Yidlish.

The so-called *mamaloshen*, the mother's or mother tongue, is especially rich in insults and imprecations: one hilarious "story" by Sholem Aleichem is simply a long list of alphabetized curses "by a stepmother." Many of the Yiddish words that have eased into American English since the 1950s are terms of disparagement. In some circles of American Jews, discussing the fine distinctions among *shmoe*, *shlep*, *shlemiel*, and *shlemazel* might be, for a moment, a nostalgic amusement. (My spell-check accepts *shlep*—probably the verb—but not the others. Transliteration is as tricky as translation.) Both the game and the distinctions suggest the importance of shades of meaning, in the disparagement department of Jewish culture, and beyond that the all-importance of language-focused, self-deprecating Yiddish humor. The worlds of Sholem Aleichem and I. B. Singer, Irving Howe's "world of our fathers," is a world of traditions, yes, but more uniquely of expressions, of language. There ought to be an analogue, apropos Yiddish, of the aphorism about a dialect with a navy: native speakers of a language that does not have roots in a national land use gesture and intonation more than most. And frequently they use words as weapons.

My parents didn't want us to learn to speak Hebrew any more than they wanted us to learn Yiddish, but they insisted that we go to Hebrew school to learn what they considered the basics, the characters of the alphabet and the prayers and the holidays—to learn how to be Jews, my father pragmatically explained, since people would take us for Jews whether we practiced or believed in Judaism or did not. To ensure that other Jews wouldn't laugh at us for being ignorant. In Hebrew school, if you were lucky, you got Mr. Spodek. Famous for throwing the odd chalk-laden felt blackboard eraser at the odd inattentive child, he was a brilliant teacher: I can no longer remember his lessons and digressions, which informed my attentiveness to words and sentences, paragraphs, and chapters. (Illustrating the difference between direct and indirect objects, he sometimes used the eraser.) For the fun of it, he read or told us stories, in English of course, about the Wise Men of Chelm. ("Spodek": memory has surprised me by washing up a name I haven't thought of for years, and suddenly I am more surprised to hear my father's voice say it reflectively, shortening and rounding the vowels into Yiddish ones. Was the Astoria Hebrew teacher also a Galitzianer? Had his ancestors, like mine, come from that low-end part of Europe where you found the rhyming neighboring villages Chelm and Belz along with half-rhyming Mielec and other late and lamentable largely Jewish towns with assonant names [like Glupbsk] hovering between German and Slavic, between history and myth? How did my father know or guess that? How do Jews whose ancestors came from those backward impoverished areas manage to recognize one another cheerfully as *landsmen* and fellow *kaptzonim* and in the act of recognizing to put the other guy down as a known and inferior quality, in a rueful parody of the family pride of people from places like Berlin and Vienna, Chernivtsi or Prague?)

The folk tales about the comical Chelmites are set in a city where all the people are Jews who—although they look like other European Jews, with long beards and caftans—are not quite like everyone else, not altogether right in the head. Either they are all fools or silly things befall them: the teller of the tales refuses to decide. Chelmites are a peculiar species of what the Germans call *Luftmenschen*. For example, when people in Chelm decide to brighten a dark room, they gather buckets of sunlight to pour into it; when their town needs a new mill, they choose to build it at the top of a hill at a scenic but impractical distance from the river that might have worked to power it; they try to steal the moon by capturing its reflection in a barrel of borscht, then quickly covering the top of the barrel so it won't evaporate. A children's book of stories about Chelm with illustrations that looked like old woodcuts was published in New York soon after the war ended, as American Jews worked to recall more distant and pleasant memories to cheer themselves up. I assumed the folkloric tales were complete fictions until I was surprised to find on a map a dot, not far from Mielec and Belz, labeled Chelm—which some people say has nothing to do with the stories.

To us, back then in Astoria, the stories of the Wise Men of Chelm—who were wise only ironically—suggested that there was something funny but somehow dead serious as well about being Jews in the first place. It also suggested by the way that Jews were good at making fun of themselves. Variations on this theme began to be elaborated, after the war, by comedians in the Borscht Belt and on the radio and television, by the Marx Brothers, and Milton Berle, and Mel Brooks, and much later by the Coen brothers and Joan Rivers and the twenty-first-century evocation of her, in *The Marvelous Mrs. Maisel*. As if in self-defense, Jewish comedians developed, after the war, the idea that there was something intrinsically if ruefully comical about the fact of being Jewish, specifically, being Jewish the way we were.

In my childhood in the pretty-much-all-white cultural melting pot of mid-century Astoria, Queens, children who were good at school and their parents openly and boastfully compared IQ scores as well as grades, while children with what are now called learning difficulties were segregated in CRMD classes (the initials, we all knew, stood for "Children of Retarded Mental Development"). Moron jokes were popular in both groups ("Why did the moron throw the clock out of the window?" "He wanted to see time fly.") Mr. Spodek knew what he was doing when he chose to enchant us with tales of the Wise Men of Chelm, who were not wise at all. Their old world was a world turned upside down, where grown men thought and behaved like philosophers and silly children.

We were going to school to become smarter, more successful, more modern, and more American than the Chelmites (or our parents). Immigrants or the children of immigrants from Europe, they were—in contrast to us—primitive, primeval, old-fashioned Jews. "The Wise Men of Chelm" were faux folktales. There was a hint of mischief in hearing them read aloud in Hebrew school: was Mr. Spodek making fun of our parents, a little? Had Jews been morons like the Chelmites for generations—until when? Was modernity, for Jews, a consequence of War, or of Revolution, or of Zionism, or of the very belated arrival in Eastern Europe of The Enlightenment, in the late nineteenth century? Or were we living in the aftermath of a surfeit of suffering that had risen like a wave and toppled some people into terrible deaths while random luckier others got across the ocean to America?

Later, of course, when I read more about the systematic near-extermination of the Galitzianer Jews in the twentieth century, that true tragic history darkened all my mental images. In my early life, the threat posed by Mielec was more inchoate. Ours was a family in which bad things were avoided and evaded, not dwelt on or even mentioned—but of course the real evils of the human condition haunted our comfortable lives. When my brother and I were little and still sleeping in the same room, we would collaboratively resolve mysteries that we sensed were being kindly kept from us. We decided that our parents were on their way to rob banks when they left us to go for a walk of an evening, as they told us. And what signals were encoded in that secret guttural language they spoke? We also decided, we thought quite brilliantly, that just as people automatically had children after they got married, they began to speak Yiddish when they got old. While this youthful conjecture has proved untrue, I have recently tried to study Yiddish—alongside mostly other elderly people—and, more successfully, to enjoy listening to Sholem Aleichem's Tevye stories read aloud and broadcast from the currently flourishing Yiddish Book Center in Amherst, Massachusetts. The cadences of the *mamaloshen* bring me as close as I can get to Mielec.

Sholem Aleichem's Tevye is a milkman-philosopher (made sense to me, as my mother's Yiddish-speaking brothers Sam and Yussele both dealt in butter and eggs and cheese). His first-person narratives about his good and bad fortune are told to "Pan Sholem Aleichem," the gentleman-Jew writer who would have no trouble getting all his literary allusions and references. Tevye's vernacular is generously shot through with Hebrew, punctuated by quotations from the Torah as well as the learned commentaries on it: *loshen kodesh*, the holy language, runs like an underground stream through his consciousness, therefore his language. This is an aspect of the realism of the stories (my father indulged in similar learned asides) and of their fantastic side, as well. It was not implausible that the humblest and poorest of European Jews might be as familiar with the Holy Book as Tevye is: every Jewish boy went to *cheder*. And it was a commonplace that a Jew like Tevye should consider his personal case, as Tevye does, emblematic of the Jewish condition. *"Vas macht a Yid?"*—How's a Jew doing?—is still a friendly greeting among Jewish men. *"S'iz schver tzu sein a Yid!"*—It's hard to be a Jew!—remains a rueful half-serious Yiddish lament, uttered with a sigh. To see yourself as a Jew above all and a representative of Jewry generally is a Jewish habit: Sholem Aleichem did not invent it.

Tevye's stories are about hard work, bad luck, family love, competition, and the struggle with the power of the *goyim*. Like the Chelmites who schemed to steal the moon, the hero is not a worldly man or a rich man but a high-minded idealist.

I was born in Beth Israel Hospital in New York City in 1937. The mass murders in Mielec that began in 1939 were not discussed in my hearing in our neighborhood of lower-middle-class immigrant Astoria, Queens, where the other families were either Jewish or Italian or Irish Catholic, with a sprinkling of Armenians, Ukrainians, and Greeks. There was one Chinese boy in my class, but no other people of color in residence. We were taught to praise America as a "melting pot," but our teachers had not yet come to acknowledge the recalcitrant hard lumps in it. "Racial and religious prejudice" was a familiar anodyne phrase in classroom lectures about tolerance, but it made me nervous, and I joked to my friends that the teachers who re-peated it were pointing a finger at me, mispronouncing my first name. While I knew that some kids and parents looked down on Negroes and Jews, I had no idea that White Protestants were the bedrock of the ruling class until I got to Barnard, where I learned the social significance of a raincoat lined with Burberry's signature plaid. Aging has a few startling gratifications: recently, I admired a beautiful young African woman wearing a head wrap printed with that plaid.

Mine was one of those 1950s families in which the word "cancer" was never said aloud, even when my aunt lay dying of it. Like most Jews of their time and place, my parents did not speak openly of the Holocaust until years after it. But I remember being taken, in the winters of the 1940s, to grim meetings of the Mielecer Relief Fund in a dark upstairs synagogue downtown that smelled of damp books, old men, and mice, where men wearing dark fedoras or yarmulkes called out the amounts of their contributions to the Fund, usually in multiples of eighteen, and made what arrangements they could to help the few Jews remaining in Eastern Europe. And I recall the strange new courteous cousins with tense pale faces and foreign accents who arrived at our house bearing oddly breakable gifts they must have carried with them for miles—a crystal bowl, a china figurine of a delicately horned bull—and told their terrible stories in whispers to my parents, in Yiddish, in the kitchen, after we had been sent to bed.

The Jews of Mielec, like the Jews of Chelm in the stories, had nicknames—often, like my sour step-grandmother Git Lucius and my father's grandmother the midwife Little Deborah, a first name plus a descriptor that was either the name of a parent or husband, or a striking trait. When Orthodox Jews marry or die they still go by their father's name, or patronymic; they never quite accepted the surnames imposed on them by the Christian world. For me, the strange names they bore helped to distance them into semi-fabulous characters, and sometimes to situate them usefully in an imagined family tree. My great-grandfather Moishidle's descendants often described one another in Yiddish—pointedly, comically, self-deprecatingly—as *"Moishidle's an ainickle"* or *"einickle,"* meaning grandchild. The phrase explained away what might seem to be quirks of character: to be my mother's grandfather's blood relation was to be by nature, as he was, demanding and difficult—ornery.

From a book published in Jerusalem in 2012, *Mielec, Poland: The Shtetl That Became a Nazi Concentration Camp,* I am astonished to learn that a 1905 census registered 2,456 Catholics in the city of Mielec and 4,017 Jews. So it was not a village or *shtetl* at all, although the Jewish section seemed to function like one, but a little city and a largely Jewish one. Jews from Mielec (including at least one member of my mother's extended family) had served in the army in World War I, and the town had had Jewish representatives in parliament. The feather-processing plants owned and operated by Jews constituted a major industry: my father's friend's family made a fortune in the feather business, a big business in Chelm, as well. The Jewish community of Mielec was prosperous enough, just before the twentieth century began, to build itself a spacious new synagogue with two towers. Buildings adjacent to the synagogue housed the *shochet* (ritual slaughterer), and the public baths and the *mikveh,* or ritual bath for women. The early Nazi atrocities were staged in 1939 in those sectarian public spaces.

In the interview that Gabriel recorded, my mother claims that her first memories of Mielec date from "after the war," when she returned with her grandmother's family in 1917 or 1918 from the town the authorities had sent them to, in Bohemia (or was it Czechoslovakia?). But she also recalls the new red cape she was wearing that tore on a nail, in Mielec, sometime before the forced exodus of 1914. And in yet another story she describes, at Gabriel's prompting, a pogrom that occurred before the war, when Cossacks on horses invaded Mielec and looted and wrecked Jewish stores and homes. When the marauders finally stopped trashing the town, they left it, leaving behind a single "Cherkass," she calls him, I suppose a Circassian, to represent their power and watch over their interests. My mother remembered him as a tall handsome man in a splendid uniform—her dazzled tone conjures respect for an icon of male power, glamor, and authority. She sketches the outlines of a horrific half-remembered incident: he was "a real handsome man, and they all got after him in town, and he was killed. Everybody took something to remember him by . . . ," she says delicately, mentioning gold buttons from his uniform but not the stickier little bits. One of her uncles was among the toughs in the lynching party.

The first time the Russians came into Mielec, the family stayed put in the bakery, and the Russians remained for about two weeks without making trouble. "One day they broke in [to the bakery], and they were getting ahold of some salt or something. My grandfather was a very thin man. My grandfather ran over, and he says, 'You're not going to get it.' Then his arm hurt him all the time. Something happened to him. . . . But the guy didn't get the salt." Another story that featured salt somehow missed being retold when Gabriel interviewed my mother. My sons and I remember Reisel recalling that one day when she had wandered some distance from her grandmother's house, some local *goyim* went after the Jews on the streets, and she was scared and a neighbor who recognized her, a Jewish lady, invited her into her house for safety. It happened to be lunchtime, and the neighbor happened to be serving her family, but she did not invite the frightened child to sit down at the table with them. Standing near the table, smelling the food and watching the others eat, hungry little Reisel reached out and slipped a finger into the salt, then licked the salt off her finger when the woman turned her back to serve the others: that was lunch, for her, that day. Telling the story, she marveled at the woman's lack of generosity—but not at the marauding *goyim*. Nor did she make a fuss about her hunger, which must have been a familiar problem.

Fearful in the face of a promised pogrom, the whole family, carrying what they could, boarded a train to get away when the war started: the Austro-Hungarian authorities helped to bundle them off. They must have expected Moishidle's family to be targeted by the Russians for a couple of reasons: because they sought to destroy the business and property of Jewish shop owners, and perhaps because they knew of the uncle who had been in the murderous mob that had lynched the Cherkass.

Her most vivid, extensive memory of Mielec is of what must have felt like her first emigration, the forced move by train to the countryside in what must have been 1914. Explaining it to Gabriel many years later, she looks back through the scrim of a more recent and familiar frightening past, now easily, if delicately, acknowledging the Holocaust: "The government took us on trains, like what we might hear about the Jews when they were taking them to those gas houses. We were just a lot of people in a train. You couldn't sit. You couldn't eat. Finally we got to our destination. It was Czechoslovakia like, but it was a very small village. The village was named Schtelkowitz; the city was named Zot. We got in wagons, and they took us, whatever bundles we brought I don't remember. All I know is that I had to go to the bathroom. I peed into the bundles, whatever, in the wagon." Gabriel asks, "How old were you?" and she answers immediately, "Nine years old." Born in 1905. "Finally we got to that place," she continues. "The man that took us in was a very rich . . . He didn't look like a Jew, they were very rich assimilated Jews." What she meant, of course, that he wasn't dressed as a Jew, or wearing a beard and *peyes*.

The Mielecer Jews stuck together in the foreign place, she recalls. "They had a *minyan*. They opened the *shul* there. They felt like at home. We went to school there. When we got there, the man gave us living quarters that his help that used to shear the lambs had lived in, he must have replaced the help or something, and we had two rooms. My grandmother had one, and my aunt and uncle had one. I don't know what happened. They must have brought beds because we took those beds back to Mielec." By "beds" she meant large quilts, featherbeds. Her father and his new wife were with the family, but she doesn't mention them at all, in the interview. But when my cousin Adrianne visited us in New York some years ago, my mother recounted the sketchy, tendentious story that once the family got to their refuge, Ahzhe and his new wife Paircha disappeared, and everyone went looking for them, and that when they found them she was pregnant! It was the first and only time I heard that story. Instinctively, my mother produced and tailored her stories for her audiences: her half sister Ruth or Roozha, Adrianne's mother, would have been the fetus.

She recalls happy, sunny days in the country village, bucolic, idyllic, and free, far from home in besieged and poverty-stricken Mielec: "We went to school there. I used to love it. We went into school early in the morning, waiting for the teacher. You know what they did? They sang the math, the table—the times table." She sings it in German, apologizing a little because "it didn't go too far, because the teacher came." You can hear her pleasure in knowing the language, and in recalling

going to school and learning: she seems to remember everything they taught her that year, and she never forgot the names
of the foreign villages.

———————

When I was nine years old, I was "promoted," as they said, from
smiling, personable, pregnant Mrs. Liberty's class to Miss
Crookes's. Miss Crookes—Florence—was thin and grim and
all business; her passion was entomology, which she scrupled
to distinguish from etymology. As she must have known some
of her pupils would be, I was thrilled to collect two such words
at once. She taught us the difference between insects and bee-
tles and other bugs: an insect has six legs and three parts to its
body, a head, a thorax, and an abdomen. In good weather, she
took us on field trips to one of the grassy cemeteries in Queens,
where we roamed—each of us carrying a glass jar with holes
punched in its tin lid so our insect would be able to breathe—
collecting caterpillars, grasshoppers, and bits of leaves and
grass for them to eat and hide in. If you were very lucky, you
would delight Miss Crookes by finding and capturing a praying mantis, an enormous, elegant insect so important that
you were prohibited by law from killing it. (If you did, Miss
Crookes would for sure send you to jail.) Front legs crossed as
if in prayer, indigenous to cemeteries, praying mantises were
spookily preying mantises as well: the female ate the male after he fertilized her eggs, we learned.

But it wasn't the spookiness that fascinated and stayed with
me, although that haloed everything with solemnity. Miss
Crookes's intellectual passion was impressive and contagious:
much more committed to her subject than to her students, she
was a wonderful teacher. But that, I think, is not the only reason why I learned for life what she taught me. Children of nine

or ten are, I think, especially vulnerable to absorbing organized knowledge: the nineteenth-century English philosophers James Mill and Jeremy Bentham worked especially hard at stuffing little John Stuart Mill with languages and declensions and conjugations, when he was around that age. What Miss Crookes taught me about insects was my first experience with organized knowledge. I still remember it, as my mother remembered, all her life, the beginning of the times table in German.

She loved living in the pretty village across the street from the church—not a Catholic church, she said, but lighter and more modern. There was a lady attached to the church who fussed over her baby cousin Dullah. She remembers the cruelly casual mischief of her younger cousin Meilach Shifras, later Mike in America, who would casually pick up one of the neighbor's baby chicks as he passed and squeeze it to death, for fun, in his hand. As I recollect this story of hers and check what records I have, I notice that Mike was born in 1913 and would have been a toddler at the time: my mother's story got distorted either by her familiarity with hearty big Mike as an adult, and/or by mine.

A happier memory of the time was of little Mike's older brother Zanvel, only a year younger than Reisel, who stole apples or cherries from a tree in a local orchard. "He climbed up and I held out my skirt for the big plump fruit," she says to Gabriel, as if reciting a children's story. It's a not unfamiliar story about city kids in the country, a timid girl's excitement about adventures with bolder boys. There is a hint, barely audible, of respect (borrowed from my father?) for reasonable German Protestant civilization, so very different from the superstitious Catholicism of Eastern Europe.

But her official first memory is of the beautiful coat or cape, in either case new and red, which accidentally got torn when she was "five years old," maybe on her way to school, because "they were building something in the street and a nail stuck out." If she remembers right, that would have been in 1910, before the First World War. I interpret this mix of fact and fiction as metaphorical: there was building going on in Mielec, in my mother's early childhood, but constructive progress didn't actually take place.

In the middle of the nineteenth century, my great-grandmother Brucha Bienenstock married Moses Judah Thaler—"Moishe Yehiedeh" in their dialect, hence "Moishidle," a diminutive for a pompous double name attached to a small man. For the rest of her life she supported him and his habit of praying in place. Their son Abraham Isaac, always called Ahzhe, was born in 1870. Brucha Thaler was admired and respected in Mielec for her probity and her character, for the way she ran her household, and for the economic and social power that accrued to her: in 1920, "B. Thaler"—the wife, not the husband—was listed as a baker in at least one official Mielec directory.

In the Bubbe Brucha's big house in Mielec there was no running water, no indoor toilet. Downstairs, on the main floor, was the bakery with its big high oven, behind the store. Living in the house with Brucha and Moishidle were their four married daughters together with their husbands and children, my mother's beloved aunts Liebe, Shifra, Sheindel, and Feige, who had helped the Bubbe bring her up. Presumably everyone slept upstairs, but the setup was never clear to me: my mother always said that she slept with her grandmother in one bed until she left for America. I have no idea where Moishidle slept. I remember being told that the *Shabbes goy* slept behind the oven, but in the recorded interview she describes Moishidle sitting on top of it all day with his holy book, looking up from time to time to make sure everything below was kosher and correct. Here's an excerpt from the transcript:

*Gabe Brownstein:* Who ran the bakery, your grandmother or your grandfather?

*Rose Mayer:* My grandfather had nothing to do with the bakery.

*Gabe Brownstein:* He had nothing to do with the bakery.

*Rose Mayer:* He didn't know a damn thing. All he knew was sitting all day studying, reading the Torah.

*Gabe Brownstein:* Stayed in the house upstairs?

*Rose Mayer:* Not upstairs. You see, the ovens were built a different way now. They used to call them the new ovens, the German ovens. The old-fashioned ovens were built with brick. We had sand there. It was warm. In the wintertime we used to climb up there. We had to climb. We had a stepladder. My grandfather used to sit there all the time. He was very thin. He never did anything. If he needed to wash his hands, if he scratched himself, he couldn't touch the holy book, so he used to scream, "Bring me a glass of water." My grandmother said to him, "Get yourself a glass of water, Moishidle, and whenever you scratch yourself you could use it. . . ." "They've got nothing better to do," he says. I used to do my homework there in the wintertime. It was warm. It was nice.

*Gabe Brownstein:* He had the nicest spot.

*Rose Mayer:* Oh, my grandfather had the holiest spot.

*Gabe Brownstein:* He could look over everybody else?

*Rose Mayer:* He was always criticizing. He had a son-in-law that was flirting with the ladies. He said to my grandmother, "I don't like the way he moves around the women there."

When my brother rented an apartment in Cambridge, Massachusetts, that featured a solitary study up a flight of stairs, my mother recognized the layout approvingly. And perhaps she was reminded of Moishidle in his sanctuary when I became impatient with the children's noise in the house in Vermont, in the summers, and she would say, a little too tactfully and sympathetically, with what I heard as notes of condescension, "Rachel dear, *mammeleh*, why don't you go upstairs and type a little?" Upstairs was for readers and writers, *Luftmenschen*, not honest plain people like her who worked with their hands: the distinction was well defined, in my family, and classed and gendered as well. That was why, the day she came upon me mopping the linoleum, she sat down hard on a chair and began to cry. "I was the brawn," she would recall, in the years after my father died; "your father was the brains." She did not want me to be like her—but on the other hand, of course she did.

According to the rabbis, serving a learned man who serves God by studying Torah is the way for an ordinary, ignorant man to serve God. And when a virtuous and learned man sits enthroned in heaven, his wife and helpmeet serves as his footstool.

The two aunts who figured in my mother's stories are the Meema Liebe and the Meema Shifra. ("Mooma" or "Meema" in the Galitzianer pronunciation means "Aunt" in Yiddish; "Fetteh" means Uncle.) There seemed to be much less to say about their husbands—ordinary, earthbound men who worked with their hands, and probably did not concern themselves much with a little girl. She loved best the Meema Shifra, the hardworking mother of the little chick-killer who turned himself neatly into big Mike in America, and of his glamorous older brother Zanvel, who, the story goes, became a Communist and fled Europe under mysterious circumstances to Argentina, where he died violently, too young, to be forever mourned by my mother as her lost best friend. He would have been her first playmate, after she was deposited in the bakery at two or three years old. I think that as a girl she had been in love with him.

She also loved the milder Meema Liebe, mother of her cousin

Yussel, always called Yussel Liebes, who many years later would open a Jewish bakery like his grandmother's bakery, in Washington, DC. She loved even more Yussel Liebes's younger sister Dullah, the child who had been adored, as an infant, by the lady at the Protestant church in Bohemia. Dullah would have been about ten when her reluctant sometime babysitter left for America. Some years after my mother left Mielec, Dullah herself immigrated to Israel, where she lived on a leftist kibbutz and—scandalizing my father—did not marry the man with whom she had three daughters until Israel became a state in 1948 and she was finally made an honest woman. In my childhood my mother sent packages wrapped in brown paper—a coffee tin filled with her own home-baked brownies, a kosher salami, a small radio—to Dullah in the kibbutz. My father warned they would be swiped by the surely corrupt communistic authorities. My mother persisted in sending the packages: she either didn't believe him or didn't care.

Did my grandfather Ahzhe Thaler expect to live permanently alongside his four sisters and their husbands and children in his parents' house over the bakery when he came back from America with his three motherless children, having left behind a healthy infant in the Jewish orphanage in New York? His sisters' husbands would have scorned the white hands of the would-be gentleman; so, more damningly, would Moishidle, who could not have been proud of a son who was not equipped, intellectually or spiritually, for high-minded pursuits. But Ahzhe was also Brucha's only surviving son—"Ahzhe," soft as a sigh, for the softie. She would have understood that the young widower was feeling sorry for himself after the long journey by steamship and train with three children, and she must have been aware there was nothing for it but another wife. He would find one: that much he was able to do. She welcomed him and his family to the already crowded house, and then gently encouraged him to find his own place. In a few weeks or perhaps months, he managed to move out with his boys: probably there was an agreeable lady loosely attached to this move, someone he might have had his eye on before he married, or perhaps a new widow. He married or didn't quite marry her: my mother was evasive on this sensitive point. When he left home this time, Brucha refused to let him take the youngest of the children he had brought back with him, the little girl who years later would tearfully recollect, as a sign of her grandmother's wisdom and greatness of heart, that she had persuaded him to leave his eldest son behind in Europe with her in the first instance ("My grandmother wouldn't let Chayim go"). The Bubbe Brucha must have been close to sixty by the time she took on the job of raising little Reisel: "Say I had another baby on my old age," my mother quoted her.

On both sides, I come from a long line of ineffectual learned men and sturdy hardworking women: cf. my father's grandfather, the *melamed* whose pupils pasted his beard to the table when he nodded out, and his tiny wife the midwife Deborah, "*die kleine Dvoirele*," who threw on her little cape and went out to deliver a Jewish baby in Mielec at any hour of the day or night. My Mayer grandfather Avrum Chayim, my father's father, didn't do much more than his father had done; neither did his younger brother Jacob, who when I knew him was also bearded, and two or three inches shorter than my short grandfather. A sardonic cousin referred to them as "the Smith Brothers," after the pair of ornamental bearded men on the American cough-drop boxes.

My father was taller than his own younger brother, my uncle Max—at five feet five, or so he claimed, he was the tallest in the family. My mother relished pointing this out sarcastically, her way of laughing at the whole little family: her voice would always move into a respectful register when she had occasion to describe "a tall, handsome man," her vowels like organ tones. Was she laughing at herself, a little, for marrying a little man? The Jews of Mielec had not been well nourished, as their tall American grandchildren would be. She remembered Moishidle himself as a skinny, dry little man, watchful and nervous and demanding, helpless and always shrieking for help. Still, when the Cossack wanted to steal salt from the family, Moishidle had stopped him, even though the guy twisted and hurt his arm. In the Orthodox communities of Eastern Europe, the scholar who devoted his days to reading the Word of God was the most admired of men. That the rich man or *nagid* was also admired is not a distinguishing characteristic of these people: the rich and powerful are admired everywhere.

My mother recalled a gritty but happy childhood from which she liberated herself by joining the Zionist movement at eleven or twelve. Zionist organizations were developing youth movements in Europe, at that time, aiming to encourage immigration to Palestine: Hashomer Hatzair established a club in Mielec around the time my mother entered adolescence. She learned songs and dances in the movement, and she recalled that the leaders and older girls taught her how to dress and keep herself and her clothing clean.

As an elderly woman my mother still could recite the Polish and Russian names of the great rivers of Europe, as she could sing the Hebrew prayers and—in several languages—the "Internationale," the working-class anthem she would have learned in the Zionist movement. In or out of school, she had acquired enough Russian and Polish to have a simple brief conversation. She knew a little German, as well: my brother tells me that she once picked up a book in his apartment and read ten pages of it before she realized it was written in German. She could read and write Yiddish and at least one European language, and I remember her enjoying showing off her smatterings of Russian, Czech, and Hungarian; she knew the prayers, proverbs, and many songs in Hebrew and Yiddish. From Sholem Aleichem and also from Grandma Rose, a proverb in Yiddish-Hebrew-English-German goes: *"Bemokem she-eyn ish / Iz a hering oykh a fish."* Freely translated this means, In a place where you can't find a decent man, they consider a herring a fish: in other words, An inadequate man will pass for a man when there's no competition with a real one, just as a herring will do where there are no proper fish. The complex beauty of this saying is first, the pairing of a Hebrew phrase from the Shulchan Aruch with a sentence in ordinary household Yiddish, and second, the rhyming of *ish*, the Hebrew word for *man*, with the Yiddish or German or English word *fish*. Cf. the related surrealist feminist maxim, "A woman without a man is like a fish without a bicycle."

When I was a little girl, at the end of the school year, before the Fourth of July, we all got in the car with our suitcases and pots and dishes and my father drove slowly and tentatively up Route 17 so we could spend the summers at a bungalow colony in the Catskills. He would drive up to join us for weekends, later, in "bumpa-ta-bumpa traffic." For years I thought that that phrase—like the word "affidavit"—was Yiddish. At Fogel's Farm, as we called it, the owners—immigrant Jews with foreign accents, probably from a place like Mielec—grew nothing but grass. We were a lively bunch of kids at the bungalow colony— my brother and I, our two boy cousins on our father's side, and their four or five cousins, all but one of those also boys, the children of the sisters of our tall, blond, saturnine aunt Anna, my father's brother's wife. We had the run of the place, but for fear of passing traffic we couldn't go off the grounds and onto the road without a grown-up. I remember leading a long line of little boys chanting a prayer for rain ("God Please Let It Rain") that also involved "whitewashing" big rocks with wetted pieces of chalk and marching around them. I have no idea why.

When you did get to walk on the road near the bungalow colony, there were only two places to go: the muddy lake we swam in that turned the new little hairs on our arms brown, and the wild overgrown field full of huckleberry bushes where my mother got filling for her pies and, invariably, poison ivy: she treated her blisters stoically by applying Clorox to them. My mother picked many more buckets of huckleberries (we were enlisted to help), made more and better pies, and got worse cases of poison ivy than any of the other women. It was a point of pride with her.

The hills around us—the Catskill Mountains—were alive with strange people unlike us, people we didn't know. There were men in dungarees who drove haying machines, like Hiya Bill, who would wave back when we shouted in chorus, "Hiya, Bill!" In addition to those *goyish* farming people, there was a group of very different-looking others, silent dark-clothed men my father jokingly, disparaging them, called cowboys, who walked on the road even on the hottest days wearing black suits and broad-brimmed fur hats. These strangers were traditional Orthodox Jews, Chassidim, members of I don't know which sect. It was the big hats—*streimels*—that made my father, in America, ridicule them as "cowboys." They were also Jews, but altogether unlike us, less like us, even, than Hiya Bill the *goy*, who waved back.

My great-grandmother the Bubbe Brucha was not a member of a Chassidic sect. So far as I know, she had not grown up in or near one of the many "courts" of rabbis where believing Jews congregated in Eastern Europe. Nevertheless, the story goes that at a critical dark point in her life—after she married Moishidle and began to have too many children, and not enough to feed them—she went on a pilgrimage to one such court, sat for hours on a hard bench along with other female petitioners, and finally, when she got her audience, she told her story—posed her problem—to the wonder rabbi. He pondered. Finally, gnomically, he advised, of course in Yiddish, "Bake bread and you'll have bread." The origin story, the tale of how the Thalers got their bakery, is rooted in Chassidism and holiness. How their women got their work ethic, which allowed Moishidle to pray all his life instead of working, is a different, longer story.

It was a very successful bakery: in its heyday the hearth was the heart of the Mielecer *shtetl*. On Fridays, it was full of Brucha's gleaming braided challahs, along with the Jewish community's *cholents* (or bean stews), which were cooking to be eaten on the Sabbath, when a pious Jew was not allowed to do any work, which included picking up a pencil to write or lighting or tending a fire. Weekdays, Brucha and her daughters and sons-in-law produced corn breads and rye breads and pumpernickels, and bagels that were boiled before baking. They braided the challahs and painted them with the whites of eggs well before the Sabbath began. There was always enough to eat, my mother recalled, comparing the lucky family in the bakery with other poorer families, acknowledging the wonder rabbi's good sense.

The conjunction of the commonplace and the magical, the banal and the mystical, the literal and the metaphorical: this is one thick thread that runs through all my mother's stories about her grandmother and Mielec—and Sholem Aleichem's stories about Tevye, as well. The Bubba Brucha, the story goes, was called in the night to visit the bed of a child choking with diphtheria, and when she laid her fingers softly on either side of the child's throat the child began to breathe. The Bubbe taught my mother never ever to sew a piece of clothing while a person was wearing it: if you did that, you sewed up the person's powers of thinking, the *saichel*. Aphorism, metaphor, abets superstition: as the Greeks also knew, women's cutting and spinning and weaving and knotting is a minefield of metaphors. They said that when a boy brought a girl home to his mother, in Mielec, the mother would toss her a skein of tangled string or wool to tease apart, to test the limits of her potential wifely patience. It sounds like something in a fairy tale, but it is in fact also a good test of the ability to deal with and organize the ties that bind. My mother was good at untangling complicated knots—she did it effortlessly, it seemed to me. Like her sturdiness and strength and capacity for physical labor, it was one of her innate qualifications for womanly excellence.

For fun she enjoyed working with string in the opposite direction, using a crochet hook to knot string into doilies and baby blankets and hats, or clicking knitting needles to turn brilliantly colored cheap acrylic yarn into booties for men and women and boys and girls, and in the end for babies someone would surely someday have. "Bed socks," a dignified high-WASP friend of mine called them once, in a thank-you note he wrote to her. Because he was a tall man, handsome and distinguished, she tried to use that term instead of "booties" to lend her handiwork dignity, but soon gave it up as too fancy. In her eighties and nineties, she made pairs and pairs of booties in electric colors, gifts for relatives, friends, and acquaintances. My brother and his wife call them "feet." I have bags of them in more than one closet—also needlepoint covers for pillows and pictures in frames, and, in drawers, tablecloths and matching napkins embroidered with cross-stitching. Women's work is never done.

# CHAPTER 4

# SHAPING NARRATIVES

Bright young guest at dinner party in the 1960s: "We're planning to vacation in Europe this summer. Have you been to Europe, Mrs. Rothfeld?—"

Dour older guest, with a strong foreign accent: "Europe? I vas born dere!"

ONE OF MY MOTHER'S FAVORITE JOKES

*Im dalej w las, tym więcej gówna.* (The deeper you go in the forest, the more shit you find.)

ONE OF MY MOTHER'S FAVORITE POLISH PROVERBS

The details varied as my mother retold the story of her life: her mood, her audience, the context, and the point she wanted to make colored what she remembered and what seemed better to conceal. In a rush of pride in her tender feeling for her younger brother Harry, for instance, she could bring tears to her eyes recalling that the very first thing she did in New York on that brisk day in March was to go with Sam by cab to visit Harry in the Hebrew Home. While it might have happened that way— I have learned that Harry was not discharged from the Home until September 5, 1924, so there would have been five months in which such a visit might be made—I suspect it did not. But for the moment, for love of her American brother and of herself loving him, she believed it had happened that way.

Her most extensive account of her life was written the evening before the solemn High Holy Day of Yom Kippur in 1983, as she sat alone in her modest condominium apartment in Florida—two rooms, a small kitchen, and a screened porch that looked out on the pool five stories below. She had enjoyed listening and singing along to "Kol Nidre" on the radio, her custom since my father died, but now she was feeling aimless and sad and already a little hungry, at the very beginning of the holiday when she always fasted the whole day. The apartment felt like the grave. She picked up a ballpoint pen and a lined notebook and wrote at the top of a page "Erev Yom Kippur, 1983." It turned out to be less of a thrill than she had imagined it would be to defy her dead husband's and her grandfather's and their God's injunction against working, which includes writing, on the Highest of Holy Days, but she wrote on, explaining she was following her "sweet daughter Rachel's suggestion" that instead of "wasting time" she should write down the story of her life for her children. My first book, about women in English novels, had been published the previous year, and in the first chapter there are a few paragraphs about my parents.

She begins as usual with the dramatic scene of her arrival in New York, but soon gets distracted from the patriotic point. "I was 18½ years old. Just looking at New York was a thrill I will never forget. Then my brother Sam took a cab and we went to visit my Uncle Ellish, he was my grandmother's favorite brother. Why? Because she nursed him at the same time with her firstborn. That was nothing special in Mielec. Maybe her mother was too busy." The syntax and word order are confusing: the writer has stumbled into telling a story that strikes her as indecorous and disloyal, and it becomes hard to follow. "Why?" I didn't understand until I read the passage a second time that she is not asking why she and Sam visited their

Uncle Ellish right away but why Ellish was their grandmother's favorite brother.

Her syntax wobbles, I think, because it embarrasses her to recall the story that her grandmother had nursed her own younger brother with her own breasts: she is embarrassed that the chaste process of writing has led her back involuntarily to Mielec and to something intimate and incestuous and uncivilized in the past of her family—evidence of suppressed Galitzianer barbarism. In the late nineteenth century, muckraking European journalists had deplored as they explored the filth and backwardness of the province, and the exploitation of women among the impoverished religious Jews there. The glitch in my mother's nostalgic memory seems, on second reading, to have something to do with that. Or perhaps she could no longer quite remember exactly what she and Sam had done first, on their first exciting day together in New York.

Or did she deliberately invoke—recall—her Uncle Ellish in the first place, writing in 1983 in Florida, in order to make her story a little different, this time? To temper the triumphant but by now banal tale of arrival ("a thrill I will never forget") by nodding to the mud she had emerged from? Had her intention been, when she wrote, to boast of having a respectable older relative already living in New York? Did she, in the act of writing, begin to have second thoughts about Uncle Ellish's respectability and even her grandmother's, as she took pains to explain away the abusive use of Brucha as a wet nurse by her own mother? The lame little joke ("Maybe her mother was too busy") falls flat. Did she think of her own mother, who had probably nursed her before she went and died? Of herself nursing her infants? Did she and Sam in fact go to visit Uncle Ellish as soon as she arrived in New York, or did they visit Harry instead; or did they take that cab to Brooklyn, as she tells Gabriel on the tape, to see Sam's married friend and to get her long brown hair cut, and to begin to turn herself into a real American? "The girls were wearing bulky white sweaters that year, and saddle shoes in two tones, and I liked that style and Sam bought me those," she recalled later. "And a pocketbook, at Wanamaker's. I didn't have underwear—I had flannel panties, and only one brassiere. There was a lady who had a store on Clinton Street, a specialty store, her husband was a doctor but he died, and Sam introduced me to that lady, and she got together underwear, panties, handkerchiefs, everything, and he paid for it."

Memories encourage other memories, true and false; they well up like tears. Picking and choosing among them creates distortions, and further distortions occur in the telling. Sitting at my laptop now, I find myself mixing up my own childhood with my mother's. Recalling her total recall of the first verses of the multiplication table as she learned it in Germany in 1914, I end by remembering fourth grade in Astoria, Queens, circa 1946, where I learned everything I still know about insects from Miss Crookes.

Comparisons may be odious, but people make them compulsively, or at least I do; one thing leads to another. We define ourselves in comparison and in opposition to other people, especially when reading and writing and reflecting on life stories. Out of the long-ago blue, right now, I suddenly hear the voice of my father's younger and shorter brother Max saying to my own younger brother Alan, while shoving forward his own several-weeks-older son in order to measure who was taller: "Okay, Palsy, back to back." (What he really said: "Okay, Pelsy, beck to beck.") He needed his boy to be taller than his brother's. Until this moment I had pretty much forgotten the overly friendly nickname "Palsy," from a then-popular song; also nearly forgotten, at the back of my mind, were the invidious compulsive measuring of the boys and the whole family's hilarious deafness to the madly reiterated Yiddishized vowel: *Mex, Elen, Pelsy, beck to beck. Medly.* When a friend asked me recently if my mother had a Yiddish accent, I answered that I can't say for sure. She always claimed she didn't have an *eccent*.

One recollection of my mother's life that lodged early and permanently in my childish mind—a picture, really—is that when she left Mielec for America she carried with her a freshly baked bread. In my mind's eye, the ghost of an image of sturdy Reisel at eighteen, with a bread tucked underneath her arm, got conflated with an image of the young Benjamin Franklin in long socks and knickers walking into Philadelphia carrying a bread the same way. How she exchanged her home-baked bread for her first brassiere was one of the stories she repeated to illustrate her eagerness to embrace modernity—without losing or lying about a past that might seem shameful. (As to the significance of breasts in these narratives, your guess is as good as mine.) As she told these stories to her children, and years later to her more curious and receptive grandchildren, some elements changed but the gist remained the same. My mother's emphasis, the burden of her tales, was always on her having always been exactly who she was, and on her energy and honesty and resilience, her plainness and respectability, her dignity, her truth to her history and to America and to herself.

Especially the last. As she saw it, a person's dignity was reinforced, indeed trumped, by truth to herself. She was as proud as a duchess to be exactly who she was. The duchess I have in mind is, specifically, Anthony Trollope's adorably generous and impulsive duchess who declares, "I am Duchess of Omnium, and I am the wife of the Prime Minister, and I had a larger property of my own than any other young woman that ever was born; and I am myself too,—Glencora M'Cluskie that was, and I've made for myself a character that I'm not ashamed of." "A character" for Glencora is both a reputation and an inner core, the distinctive self she had chosen to make herself.

The beauty part of it (to use a favorite phrase of my mother's) is that Reisel had done Glencora one better by being true to herself without the benefits of rank or status, birth and wealth. She had made for herself a character she was proud of having invented and sustained: that was what she had done with her life.

Early on, our mother told us about her childhood in the way of business, the didactic business of mothering—stories about the poor children in Europe, of which she had been one, who didn't have the fresh vegetables and country air we took for granted, in America. Later, she recalled anecdotes from her past as we all tended to do in our house, as a mode of conversation. When things were going well, and the four of us were together at dinner or after it, the aim was to entertain, usually with stories about other people's absurdities. Eleanor Roosevelt is supposed to have said that great people talk about ideas, ordinary people talk about events, and small-minded people talk about people. While I respect Eleanor Roosevelt, because I incline toward the novelists I disagree.

My mother was a mistress of the dismissive moral judgment: she classified people she disliked with a single Yiddish word, as for instance a *faltche* (a false or two-faced person), a *kalte* (a cold, unresponsive person), or a *ligner* (a liar). Talking about people that way to her children was in her view a mode of instruction. Liars were the worst kind of people to get involved with, but cold people and false ones—the pretentious and self-important—were also dangerous to know. One of the most dangerous kinds of people was an *oyssgerechenter*, a calculating character who kept one eye always on his or her own interests. A friend like that—a person who was not motivated by feeling and impulse and generosity, as well as virtue—was bound to betray you in a pinch, or even before that.

The kind of smug woman my mother smilingly called a *fency crecker*, who condescended to her, was another species of moral monster—but if the *crecker* in question found my mother adorable, that was another matter. And a talented and charming liar, male or female—in Yiddish, *a ligner mit an oirinkel*, or earring, that is, an inveterate, elaborate liar—could elude her snap judgment if they were funny and seemed self-aware.

All my life I have been in awe of her ability to assess and judge people quickly, to sum them up with an epithet that cut them out of her life once and for all; in contrast, I in confusion weighed interesting faults against irritating virtues, and blurred clear distinctions between simple categories. "What do you need her for?" she would say to me of a friend who had hurt my feelings. Although her choice of words pained me—as it did when she dismissively pronounced, "I have no use for her"—my mother was not in fact talking about making use of other people. Of course, like the rest of us, she did use the people around her for all kinds of purposes, especially subject matter.

Like all happy enough families, we were mindful of one another's sensitive corns and allergies. The general rule of family conversation was to avoid even the semblance of putting someone on the spot, to say nothing my father could term "personal." I knew my new husband would never fit in with the four of us when he mentioned for the second time, in the course of a story he was telling about a pleasant vacation, that he had eaten a shrimp salad sandwich (not kosher), causing my father—who did not give a fig what the man ate—to grimace and mutter, "Again he tells me about the shrimp salad." Pointing to the differences among us or even acknowledging them was out of bounds in the family game of laughing at the neighbors, telling new stories about them or, better yet, recalling old ones.

Mocking other people was the way we reinforced our own cozy sense of camaraderie—coterie, really. Someone would recall a favorite story so all of us could revel in recalling together, for example, fat Florence from the country floating on the lake sublimely, belly up, her big black bathing suit gleaming wetly like a giant inner tube; or Little Evelyn with the Two Crooked Feet, at the bakery on Steinway Street in Astoria; or the sneezing mailman who was afraid of dogs; or even Fluffy, the next-door neighbor's ingratiating pet, who was not much of a dog for the obvious reason: what kind of name was that for a dog? My mother's old stories would bubble up to increase the fun as we laughed together at people's peccadilloes: Moishidle shaking his little fist back in Mielec, cursing someone with eighty-eight good years, or boisterous Sam Thaler bounding merrily into their refugee cousin Naftali's spotless little fur shop in Corona, Queens, loudly singing, "*Alle Deitchen shtinken!*" and terrifying poor frightened Nafti, who begged him, "Sem! Pliss! You are ruining my business!"

When we children became more interested in our own lives than our parents', so did they. Because we went to (separate, gendered) high schools in Manhattan, they didn't know our friends or their families. To let them feel involved and also to keep them at their distance, we let fall crumbs from the high tables of our cosmopolitan social feasts—while keeping to ourselves the leading characters and most compelling features of our new lives. From exotic Manhattan we brought home to Kew Gardens Hills tales calculated to interest them: about my friend with the heavy foreign accent and her twin sister who spoke English perfectly, who had both been hidden in a cellar in Poland during the war; or Alan's friend Myron the Pole, the mere mention of whom tickled my parents because Myron of course was not a Pole but another child of Jewish refugees from Poland. We were raised to mimic our parents' Chelmic style, to imagine a Chelm-like world peopled with comical characters: long after we had moved from Astoria to Kew Gardens Hills my mother would recall, when the weather was bad, my brother's fifth-grade classmate Nicky Maroosis, who wore two pairs of corduroy pants at once on a cold day. Or, if I bought a dress she admired, she might remember her Astoria nemesis Mrs. L., who had enviously remarked about how nice I looked in an outfit I wore as a child—my mother had bought it on sale in the Lilliputian Bazaar at Best and Company on Fifth Avenue—"I thought it was the doctor's little girl!," in perfect and mnemonically useful iambic pentameter. Bonding in our shared contempt for this status-conscious foolish former neighbor, we would feel even more like a family.

The refugee Jews we encountered in high school, the differently exotic Jews in our college classes, were of especial interest to my parents, who were curious about the academically talented children of Sephardic and Hungarian Jews, Jewish professors and musicians, famous Jews, Jewish women lawyers, and doctors, and even Chassidim from Brooklyn. Pleasantly, to please one another, we measured ourselves against these mostly more "high-class" kinds of people. Once, after a school play, I introduced my mother to the mother of a friend of mine with a misleadingly not-Jewish surname, a self-important educated lady who for some reason coyly confided that she was known for her letters—which fatuous claim came up whenever I named my friend: "Her mother is known for her letters, is that the one you mean?" To ourselves, on a good day, the four of us looked pretty good—American Jews, just as good as anyone else, maybe better.

My mother imagined her life as first of all the story of her triumphant return to America. *Immigration* might not be the right word. Was it rather *emigration* or *migration*, or even *coming home* to the city where she had been born, where two brothers awaited her? In one of Sholem Aleichem's stories, a family traveling from Russia to America stops for a time in London, where they are gratified to encounter some Yiddish speakers and an astonishing variety of herring, food of the Jews. Surprised to find such familiar creature comforts in the land of Disraeli, as they think of it, they cheer themselves by promising one another that New York, in America, will be an even better place for them.

Questions of and about immigrants and immigration have become more complex, politically and socially, in the course of the twentieth century and into the twenty-first: for one novelist's view of the situation, see, for example, Mohsin Hamid's *Exit West* (2017), which probes the surreal dimensions of moving from one nation and kind of life to another. And for comic relief consider the case of my granddaughter Clara, daughter of my son, a US citizen, and his Canadian wife. Clara was born in Italy, where there is no birthright to citizenship, and taken "home" to San Francisco for the first time in 2004 at not quite one year old—and detained at the airport there for hours, in an age of anxiety. Although she was equipped with a Canadian passport—easier to get in Bologna than an American one, the year she was born—the baby did not have the requisite green card.

List the differences between emigration and immigration and migration *tout court*; mix well and add for good measure the so-called right of return to Israel, for Jews but not Arabs. Think about how immigrants from the same place tend to crowd together, measuring themselves against one another as if they were related. With a broad vaudevillian Italian accent, my mother used to tell a story about stout black-garbed Mrs. Sforza, whose sluggish son Vito was in my class, arguing to the school principal that her boy was just as clever as another classmate who had been placed in a "special progress" class: "Iffa Robert DeVenuto can-a skip a year-a school, why-a can't-a my Vito?" Mrs. S. wasn't anywhere near so competitive with the Irish or the Jewish mothers, is my point. "Each to his own," my mother used to say, in the ineffectual melting pot of mid-century Astoria.

In 2019, in a small city in Sweden, I met an ambitious, chic Chinese woman, a successful designer of video games, who had emigrated in search of a better life not once but twice, together with her husband and their young daughter. She had most recently relocated from America to Sweden: she explained that she had hated Los Angeles because there were too many Asian Tiger Mothers there.

The new globalism has changed the experiences of immigration and emigration only superficially. Chain migration is nothing new. In a new country, migrants still look for and find and befriend and employ and live among people who look and talk and cook and pray like themselves. My parents, who grew up unknown to each other in the same social class in the same Orthodox Jewish community of the same small city in Eastern Europe, encountered one another for the first time on the Lower East Side of New York.

What's the difference between an exile, an immigrant, and a refugee? An exile, I think, is a person important enough to be banished from a country; the princely poet Nabokov is routinely described as an *émigré*. I am embarrassed today to recall my *choizik-macher* parents' tasteless nonce word, half-derisive and half-tragic, coined in the 1940s: "refuge-Jew," which suggests that the refugees from Europe were nothing more or less than, plainly and simply, Jews.

Should one use another word entirely—simply *moving*—to denote what my parents did in the first flush of postwar prosperity, when they journeyed east from a three-room apartment in Astoria to a newly built row house—"a private house"— in Kew Gardens Hills or Flushing, according to the post office, in Queens, at a time when many families from Manhattan and Brooklyn and the Bronx that were sociologically, economically, and ethnically much like ours were doing the same thing—as families with less money and status were moving into the neighborhood we left? Was that not also a kind of mass migration, within the geographical boundaries of not only America but New York City? By the time our family settled there, Kew Gardens Hills (a real-estate dealer's amalgam of two classy Anglo names of older neighborhoods in the area, "Kew Gardens" and "Forest Hills") was almost entirely populated by lower-middle-class Jewish families like ours. We moved to the little house with the pine-paneled finished basement where we kept our television set in the period when our richer friends and relations were moving farther out on Long Island to posher residential compounds with names like "Jamaica Estates North" and the classily spelled "Rockville Centre," or north of the city to Westchester County, which a friend of mine from Brooklyn mocked as "the land without the sidewalks." Hard to say what determined the moving: postwar prosperity and herd instinct or specific desires—for privacy for their growing children, or just to do what people like them were doing, and stick with their own kind. And what about my parents' last move together, to the mostly Jewish condominium in Florida, after they sold the house in Queens to more recent immigrants in the late 1960s?

———

Both my parents were interested all their lives in discovering new American links to the "home" they had left behind. I was startled by how delighted my father was when he learned that a new friend of mine was the son of a man from Mielec he knew and had "dealt with," as he put it, downtown. It interested him to discover that some of his children's upscale friends had humble backgrounds.

At some point after 1954, the year my brother and I were sent off on the subway to be educated and assimilated at Columbia University, he was delighted to repeat gossip he had heard about the distinguished intellectual Lionel Trilling, the first Jew to be tenured in the Columbia English department. Professor Trilling was an influential literary critic, a handsome man noted for a fastidious demeanor and tweedy wardrobe indistinguishable from those of an Oxbridge don. Outsiders unaware of his early work for a Jewish publication were often surprised to learn he was a Jew. As a student at Barnard, I admired his mellifluous essays, but also amused myself in my family's way by mocking the Jewish professor's excessive Anglophilia. My father's gossip pointed toward a further wrinkle: he had heard that the professor's parents frequented, or once had, a kosher hotel in the Catskills that catered to people like my parents, who came from backward places in the obscure east of Europe—in a word, Galitzianers, despised by other Jews as horse thieves.

In fifty years and more of hobnobbing with English professors, including many who wrote about the novels of Jane Austen, as both Lionel Trilling and I did, I have frequently been asked what Trilling's name had been "originally." But I have never met anyone other than my parents who recognized it as a Jewish name. In German, and in Yiddish as well, a *Trilling* is one of three as a *Zwilling*, or twin, is one of two, they assured me. Idly, I wonder what difference it might have made to his reputation and literary criticism more generally had his surname been "Triplet." As for "Lionel," it does not seem so very rarefied to me. My parents named my brother "Alan" (in Hebrew, "Isaac") after his dead grandfather Ahzhe (or Abraham Isaac) Thaler, who already had had my two cousins Alvin piously named after him, in America. To further distinguish their son, and because his paternal grandfather was still living, they gave him "Lionel" as a middle name, an English version of the second part of the noble leonine moniker of his maternal great-grandfather, the resonantly named Moses or Moshe Yehudah (think "Lion of Judah"), in their kind of Yiddish Moishe Yehiedeh, the skinny irascible scholar known, in the Galitzianer accent with an added diminutive, as Moishidle.

Could it be that Lionel Trilling was not just a Jew but a Galitzianer? As a French poet might put it: Lionel Trilling, *mon semblable, mon frère!*

———

My mother told slightly different anecdotes to explain why she decided to leave home for good and travel alone to New York in 1923–1924. As people—as opposed to historians—tend to do, she always portrayed the decision as a brave personal choice like a choice in a novel, underplaying the broader social and economic factors that underwrote her move: increasing antisemitism in Eastern Europe, lack of opportunity, the vogue for emigration among poor people. Her brother Sam had gone back to live in America at seventeen, in 1913. Ahzhe Thaler had sought a better life in America years before that. Small wonder that his energetic daughter was ready to try her luck there years after he did.

After the end of World War I, impoverished Jews from Eastern Europe poured into the United States. One person's move encourages another's; Jews from Mielec (and similar towns) might well have anxiously anticipated the racially motivated

Immigration Acts the American Congress would pass in 1921 and 1924. Rumors that such laws were in the works may have been one reason why Abraham Isaac Thaler had written to the authorities in Washington, DC, in 1919, requesting documentary proof of American citizenship for his American-born children and for himself. While the birthright of Yussele and Reisel was recognized, his own claim seems to have been denied.

When she talked about her decision to come to America, my mother didn't mention that letter. Neither did she acknowledge the two important events in her personal life that had to have helped her on her way out: the deaths of her male protectors, such as they were, her father Ahzhe and then his father Moishidle, in 1922–1923. She did mention, in passing, the small inheritance with which her brother Sam, already in New York, could buy her a steamship ticket to mail to Mielec. But that economic detail was incidental to her focus on her social position in the Bubbe Brucha's bakery: she was telling her story and revising it, after all, as a way of figuring it out, trying to formulate and sort out her feelings and motives and relations to other characters in it. Doing so, she used the techniques that Sigmund Freud, some twenty years before she left Mielec, had ascribed to the unconscious in its work of dreams: condensation and displacement. Or perhaps, since she never read Freud, it is I who project those techniques onto my version of her.

My grandmother didn't want me to go to America, she recalled late in life, but she didn't try to hold me back. She saw she was getting old and other people were taking over the bakery, everyone wanted to be the boss. The uncles were competing with one another and with one of the cousins, Yussel Liebes, a brash boy her age with an unpleasant creaky voice she didn't like. He was a clever lad; most people admired him. Telling the story, she did not actually say but somehow managed to convey that his mother the Meema Liebe might have had her eye on Reisel as a wife for this boy; neither did she mention that her own father—the man who had left his baby in the orphanage in New York City—had flat-out refused her when she had gone to ask for sanctuary in his house, where the half sister who had replaced her was living along with two stepsisters. *"Fuhr kan America!"* he had unforgettably advised her. Skirting the commonplaces of social and economic history as well as psychological theory, trying to stop short of betraying family and personal secrets, she kept the focus on things, real objects that her narrative filled with meaning.

In the first version I heard of the story, the version adapted for children or perhaps the Young Adult version, it is a cold morning in the big room with the oven in the bakery. Steaming breath, steaming coffee. A wooden crate of eggs recently delivered and well packed in shredded paper stands at one side of the room. Casually but carefully, Reisel places her foot on top of it and leans in a little to tie the lace of her shoe. Suddenly her cousin Yussel Liebes, crazily protective of the eggs—his eggs, just delivered to his bakery—hurls his hot cup of coffee at her with an angry curse. She ducks just in time; the cup crashes and breaks, coffee splatters on the wall. Frightened by his violence, convinced that her angry cousin has won their covert battle to inherit the Bubbe's bakery, Reisel decides on the spot to leave for good. She takes a pencil, she finds a girlfriend, they sit together on a staircase, and she writes a letter telling her brother Sam that she wants to, needs to come to America. Right away. And that was that. The die was cast. In fact, in real life, it took her over a year to leave.

Early on, I imagined this scene as the culmination of a long story of quasi-sibling rivalry in which Reisel and Yussel Liebes, the cleverest and most hardworking of the Bubbe Brucha's grandchildren, vie for the Bubbe's love and the bakery with it. Reisel is hands down the most loved grandchild, but Yussel is also bright and energetic, and pushy and furthermore a boy. And unlike Reisel, Yussel has a mother—the Bubbe's daughter, the Meema Liebe—to support his claim. Early on, I saw the situation as a variation on the marriage plot, with Yussel Liebes as the unappetizing suitor and Reisel as the headstrong heroine. Jane Austen wrote more than six variations on that plot, the premise of which is that between sixteen and twenty-seven a girl is obliged to choose or reject a man once and for all, for life—that that choice is the story of her life.

By seventeen, Reisel must have seemed to the people around her ready for marriage, whether or not they read novels. No one cares for girls until they are grown up, Jane Austen observed: the aunts in the bakery, Brucha's daughters, had begun to care about this one. Not that she was a bargain: dowerless, effectively parentless, she had only herself to offer. But that was not nothing. She was strong, healthy, capable, and built to bear children; she was cheerful and charming; she might be a useful wife for one or another of their sons. Even Jane Austen found cousins in love a likely and interesting subject: see *Mansfield Park*.

Reisel's beloved gentle Meema Liebe, the mother of this aggressive Yussel, might have imagined such a love story: she liked Reisel. And she had faith in her intelligent son's ability to support a wife. But alas, Yussel Liebes was nothing like my mother's favorite among the cousins, the good-looking, athletic Zanvel, the Meema Shifra's dashing older son, who had climbed trees and thrown down apples that filled her apron when they were kids in Bohemia or Czechoslovakia. Zanvel had danced the *hora* along with her at jolly meetings of the exciting new Zionist youth group, Hashomer Hatzair, in Mielec.

I imagined that Yussel Liebes would have resented Reisel for having no interest in him, and that therefore in a mindless rage, provoked by what seemed to him her unwarranted ease in the household, he threw the hot cup of coffee at her.

The hot cup of coffee was a constant in the story my mother reiterated for many years. I remember my young children asking, Did he throw the whole cup with the coffee in it or just the coffee, Grandma? Was there milk and sugar in the coffee? And was there a saucer too? She would claim that she couldn't remember everything: too many details, too long ago, what difference does it make. But the story seemed believable to me, partly because my mother always insisted on her own coffee being impossibly hot: at a lunch counter, she would always demand a little more really hot coffee, if you don't mind, please, after a first tiny sip. The message of the coffee story was clear enough: she was in hot water, at home, unless she married this angry Yussel (there are two additional significant Yussels in her life, my uncle Joe, her next older brother, and the man she would marry, my father). And marrying this Yussel was clearly impossible for a connoisseur of male character and beauty, like her. She had to leave.

But in the interview Gabriel recorded in the 1990s, she suggests a different and more sinister story about the crate of eggs, the shoe, and the violence. This time there is no hot coffee, and the aggressor is not a boy but a man. The setting, too, is colder, not indoors but in the bakery's yard, where the crate of eggs had just been delivered. "I had a brush," she begins it, with her characteristic stalling tactic of focusing on an object—a brush to clean her shoes with, she means. Just as in the expurgated version, she puts up her foot on the wooden crate; but now as she bends over to brush her dirty shoe, she thinks she feels someone or something brushing up against her behind. Startled, she slips forward a little—and hears an ominous crack, of wood or maybe eggshells. Dead silence proves that others heard it too. Then one of her uncles—was it he who had brushed up against her, the brute that her grandfather had suspected of moving around the women too easily?—strides over and suddenly slaps her face hard, giving her a black eye. The bruise lingered for days.

Darker story; heavier assailant. Angry and humiliated, red-faced, and aching from the slap, she decides then and there to leave for America: she takes that pencil, collects the supportive girlfriend, and writes to the brother she has not seen for years, pleasant Sam Thaler on Duane Street in New York.

There was no longer a place for her in Mielec. She had no home in her hometown; her fading grandmother was unable to protect her, and her father didn't care to, then couldn't. Who could she look to for help but her nine-years-older brother Sam? He was already in New York, working in the wholesale egg business, and there was also another unknown American little brother in the Hebrew Home: she had family there. She had, as well, an official letter from Washington, DC, that said she was entitled to an American passport. And she had in a pocket a little money her grandfather had given her on his deathbed, telling her nobody had to know about it. And there was some more money to her credit in America, as it happened—her portion of her dead mother's inheritance. The plot of her life was thickening, and she was moving toward its climax.

Reisel had been thinking about leaving home for a long time, perhaps even since 1914, when she and the whole family had fled on the train because of the war—a rehearsal that proved it was possible for people to get out of Mielec for good. She felt boxed in. For an Orthodox Jewish girl in an Eastern European *shtetl*, daily life was hemmed round by even more than six hundred thirteen rules and prohibitions. A girl didn't wear short sleeves; a girl didn't run or jump rope; a girl didn't whistle. When the girl is gifted with exceptional vitality and she is good at jumping rope and beginning to glory in her body as Reisel was at around twelve, this becomes a problem, or she does. Returned from the pleasures of plundering fruit trees and oppressing baby chicks at the end of the war, Reisel was not happy to be home in Mielec. She went to school, but not regularly or enthusiastically. She continued to haul sacks of flour and barrels of water for the bakery, to sleep with her grandmother in one bed, to be awakened at night to massage her grandmother's painfully swollen legs and feet. But after the fresh air and open fields and relative freedom of the country, the city and the nosy watchful neighbors had seemed even dimmer and dirtier, and more restrictive. Physically and intellectually, she was restless.

Reisel discovered Jewish nationalism or Zionism at the biologically critical moment, with the help of organizers who had recently come to Mielec to encourage *aliyah* or immigration to the Holy Land, Palestine. Their message appealed to her hopefulness and energy: escape the old world and create a new one. Boys and girls together, singing and dancing in circles to the point of breathlessness, they would work hard to make the desert bloom, and live communally as equals, brothers and sisters, and raise their children together—as the families in the bakery had done. The Jews would become a normal nation among nations in the world, no longer cringing and hiding in fear of the *goyim*; no longer would they be pale and studious and dressed in black, keeping men and women separate from one another. In khaki shorts and open-necked shirts they would work together, tilling their own soil. They would be free of outmoded customs and laws and strict observance of the Jewish week and fasts and festivals, free from the stern laws governing food and drink and sex and marriage—there was thrilling talk of free love, in Zion!

Her Orthodox grandparents were opposed to Zionism. On the sly then, without their consent or knowledge, she (probably with Zanvel) joined a lively group of young people and embarked on hikes and study groups—"boys and girls together," she always recalled when she told the story to us, appropriating the lyrics of "The Sidewalks of New York." She learned there to talk openly about politics and religion, to sing and dance the *hora*, to wash herself and her menstrual rags. She made friends with people her family didn't know and learned a little about the world outside Mielec, and thought about issues, values, conflicts, and pleasures her grandparents did not imagine. On the verge of womanhood, she began to distance herself from their medieval household, where the laws were strict and the joys were few, and people deferred, or pretended to defer, to a tiny, bearded, demanding old man.

Hard to know what Reisel imagined about her future, back then; hard to imagine what her feelings and motives and actions really had been, after the cracked-egg crisis; hard to know if she went to America rather than to Palestine because of Sam and the small inheritance, or because New York was her birthplace.

During one of our recent telephone conversations, I tell my brother that I am writing down our mother's stories. I'm trying to put the pieces together, I explain, trying to collate what fragments I recall and, if I can, to figure out what happened and when. "Well, we know one thing for sure," he says, confidently solving my problem. "We know exactly when she got on the boat for America, because we know the date Harding died."

He was recalling the legend she liked to repeat, that on the verge of her transatlantic voyage she went to Warsaw only to find that the American Embassy was closed because President Harding had died. But a quick look at Wikipedia tells you that Harding died in a hotel room while his wife was reading him a story from the *Saturday Evening Post*, in August 1923. My mother arrived in New York harbor in March 1924, having left Bremen on March 8. "*Abfahrt von Bremen achten Merz, Presdend Roswelt. Thaler,*" says the radiogram she saved that went from "Mielec 12" to "Thaler 172 Duane N.Y."

Gabriel's interview clears things up only a little: preparing to go to America required at least three separate journeys by train, one as early as August 1923, perhaps, and certainly a later one on February 4, 1924, which is the date on the passport from the Legation of the United States of America signed by the Chargé d'Affaires in Warsaw. It identifies her as Reisla Feiga Thaler, born in New York City, New York, on April 28, 1905. A small black-and-white photograph supplements the physical description: 18½ years old, five feet three inches high, brown eyes and hair, straight hair and nose, round chin, low forehead, normal mouth, no distinguishing characteristics.

She probably had to make another trip to Warsaw to pick up the passport, and another to Krakow to get the money Sam wired her from New York. Finally, there was the last trip across the border to Bremen, in Germany, and the ship waiting there. Which must mean that there may have been as many as three big loaves of farewell bread.

"My cousin Yussel Liebes always gave me a bread when I traveled," she matter-of-factly begins her story about the passport, on the tape, quite as if she had been a habitual traveler and this cousin had never thrown anything at anybody—which may well have been the case. "When I went to America, he gave me a great big bread. I had a little, not a suitcase, a little straw thing, a bag. I got there [to the passport office], and they were very nice to me. You know, when they see a young girl" (reflecting complacently on her youthful beauty and charm, which if you believed her had been considerable). "I spoke Polish very well. I said, 'I have to go home tonight, the same night. My grandmother said that I can't sleep over.' It was snowing that day too." Triumphantly, "I got the passport." After a dramatic pause, she goes on: "Then I took the train back to Mielec. What do I know which train? I sat in the wrong train. A man passed, so I asked him if the train is going to Mielec. He said, 'No, you come with me.' I went with him, and I went to the right train, and I came home. My grandmother was so proud of me. She was so proud that I did that. O my god, it was wonderful."

Maybe she knew that part was wonderful because her grandmother praised her for being a good girl and a brave girl, as she had been raised to be. But surely her grandmother had instructed her to refuse invitations from strange men, and not to board trains with them when invited to! Maybe her memories of the first, thrilling move away from home obscured and obliterated easier later journeys. Certainly, it makes psychological and dramatic sense that this dramatic memory remained most vivid: Reisel's venturing forth on a journey from her obscure city to the center of power only to find the door closed because the president of the United States of America has died! And then managing to get them to open the whole place just for you! Even without all the nice men who were so nice to a young girl carrying a big bread, a Jewish girl who could speak Polish so well, the startling conjunction of an obscure life and the international public life, of personal and political history, would be memorable. Presumably it was recorded somewhere that they opened the American Embassy in Warsaw, that day, just for Reisel Thaler!

She liked to tell the story of that stage of her journey to America, and she often changed it a little in the telling. She tended to leave out the less dramatic elements—for instance, the useful letter that authenticated her claim to a US passport. The rules for naturalized citizenship, drawn up in 1906, were still loose: after the war, in response to his inquiry, Ahzhe Thaler had been advised that he could get a passport for himself only if he managed to execute "a satisfactory affidavit overcoming the presumption of expatriation which may have arisen against you." I don't know whether he ever attempted to get such an affidavit for himself. But because I have the document, I do know that the Third Secretary of the American Legation in Warsaw responded on November 13, 1919, to Mr. Abraham Eisig Thaler, of Mielec, Galicia, the official decision that "your son, Reisel Feige Thaler, was born in New York City on April 28, 1905, and is thus entitled to receive an American passport." Without that letter, she would not have managed to make her move.

She vividly recalled the first stage of the voyage to America, beginning with the trip overland to the German port of Bremerhaven, some five hundred miles from Mielec: "The Meema Shifra took me until the border. She bought me a smoked fish. And I had a big bread that my cousin baked for me to take along. I'll never forget when she said goodbye to me: she let out such a yell. I told it to my cousin Meilach Shifras a few years ago. She started to cry terribly. She raised me," she adds. Loaves and fishes work miracles.

"She let out a yell": she always told it that way, the older woman yielding like an animal to the cry of pain she can't suppress. "She raised me" is a belated addition: usually her grandmother gets all the credit for that. "I told it to Mike a few years ago": Mike would have been moved by the story of his dead mother's emotion, and his having been told the story and his having been moved by it would sanction his cousin Reisel's story as a real story, a true one.

What she leaves out, every time, are the feelings of the eighteen-year-old girl, tenderly raised for all her talent for hard work, who is leaving home for good. I remember asking my mother how she felt about leaving her grandmother, knowing she would almost certainly never see her again. She dodged the emotional bullet. "I showed you the silver dessert spoons, not silver plate but real sterling silver, that she sent me when I got married," she would say, and if we were home she would run to bring out the velvet-lined wooden box she kept them in, along with her best dinner service of silver plate. Every time she opened that box, it surprised her to see how few were left: "I've thrown out almost all of them, mixed them up in the garbage. Look, there were a dozen, and now there are only these left," she would marvel, not acknowledging either guilt or sorrow. Although objects signified importantly in her narratives, things of value were not very important to her in her life, except insofar as they had meaning, and especially when she gave them away.

This may be the place to recall the dramatic domestic scene I deliberately made at twelve or so, when I announced to my mother that I had gotten my period for the first time. In a clumsy attempt at intimacy and emphasis, as well as to underscore the importance of the event, I solemnly placed my hands on her shoulders first, as a sweet mother in a book I'd been reading placed her hands on her daughter's shoulders before delivering momentous news. (I think the book was *Little Women*; and yes, I was fully aware of the role reversal as I engineered it.) She quickly got the point, shook it off along with my hands, and immediately ran off to open the deep bottom drawer of the dresser where she stored her white stacks of sanitary napkins. No ideas but in things; and no acknowledgment of emotions but in things or through them.

Conversationally, she ran from one thing to another, as her

quick needle had run from hat to hat, in the millinery factory, fixing a feather here and tightening a piece of braid there. As an old woman, she was always busy, quilting or knitting with gnarly hands when she could no longer move rapidly around the house to plump pillows and dust knickknacks and straighten the framed photographs on the tables. My mother could never speak about loss or painful feelings without tearing up and going mute. Distancing, which included storytelling, kept her brave and good and optimistic. In the years after my father died, she frequently dreamed about him, she told me—but she never could see him. She said that last with wonder but also resentment, deploring the finality of death. Me, I don't dream about my mother—but I can sometimes nearly hear her.

---

In the version of her life story recorded in her nineties, she comes clean for the first time about something she had never mentioned, the humiliating delousing process she had to go through in a hotel in Germany before boarding the *President Roosevelt* for America. Because she had never mentioned it before, I do not know many things I would like to know about this episode, for example, how she was instructed to go to the hotel and by whom, and whether the official fear was of disease or poverty or simply of poor people from poor countries. Did attendants wash her and the others in the baths there? Did they use special delousing combs with narrowly spaced teeth and/or smelly toxic shampoos? Were there orderly lines, as there would be later, for the gas chambers, and a paramilitary team of attendants and inspectors? Were the people in charge Germans—proto-Nazis—or were they Americans? Was the shipping company or the government underwriting the process? Which government? Were all Jewish passengers subjected to these attentions, or only the ones with low-priced steamship tickets? Who got to decide, and how? Surely the humiliation was not required of wealthy passengers. I imagine vast tiled baths in a basement—specifically, I guess, the swimming pools in Budapest that my son, my mother's eldest grandson Daniel, would photograph and email to me nearly a hundred years later. Did the men and women get deloused separately, and did they wear swimsuits, and how did she get one, and where and how did she put it on? What about delousing pubic hair?

My mother had told me triumphantly that she had traded her bread for a brassiere at the beginning of her journey to America, and I had always imagined that the trade with another woman occurred in a cabin they shared on board the ship: it turns out that it happened before they boarded the *President Roosevelt*, while undressing for the delousing bath at that hotel. Reisel must have marveled at the useful contraption, and its enterprising owner must have proposed to exchange it for the bread, which she then sold to a grocer in town. I can understand why my mother cut the grocer out of the story, when she first told it. The truth may set you free, but it doesn't necessarily improve your narrative.

---

She remembered the long voyage and eating too much the first day at sea and being seasick all the way across the Atlantic, and her shipboard romance with a lovely family—a mother and several children on their way to join their husband and father, who was a cantor in a synagogue in New York. Like the nice man who showed her which way to go on the train in Poland, these higher-class strangers took care of her, bringing her broth and tea. It seeps out, somehow, that the eldest son was her age, and that he seemed interested in her—was this a first, tantalizing possibility of exogamy and middle-class respectability? The lovely family wrote down their name and address and gave her the piece of paper, she recalled. I don't think she ever saw them again.

———

The critical domestic events that determined my mother's emigration occurred within a few years. At some point after the war, in 1917 or 1918, things started to go badly for her in the bakery—the Bubbe Brucha was ailing, the others struggling for control—and Reisel actually went to ask Ahzhe, very carefully and probably obliquely, what she should do and whether she could live with him and his new family, Paircha and her two girls and her own half sister, Roozha. Her cold father, breaking her heart, advised coolly, "*Fuhr kan Amerika.*" Go to America. In other words, No room for you here.

But there is another way to consider the story. Being born in America made her different, she always knew: did it also suggest, to her father as well as to her, that her different destiny was to live there? Perhaps when Ahzhe Thaler cruelly turned her down he was simply pointing her in the direction that had been from the beginning *bashert*, inevitable, fated, and right.

As it turned out, even if he had agreed to receive her into his household, Reisel would not have been able to live with her father for long: in 1922 he died. His father Moishidle died the following year. The Bubbe Brucha was still alive when Reisel left Mielec, and she didn't die until after Reisel got married, in 1933, when the Bubbe mailed her the dozen sterling silver dessert spoons that my mother managed to throw out one by one by accident, so that there are now fewer than half a dozen in the shabby velvet-lined wooden box on the top shelf of my closet. The Bubbe was clear in the head till the very end, my mother used to boast as if she had been there herself to witness her dying, clear enough mentally to send Meilach Shifras, then still in residence, out of the house. On his father's side Mike was a Kohane, a member of the priestly caste and therefore forbidden to stay in the house with a dead body.

The former chick-killer had the good luck to be married by an American Jewish woman who was shopping for a husband in Mielec, and he went to America with her just in time to escape the Holocaust. I asked, but my mother never could tell me exactly when the Bubbe died. She felt all her life, as she had felt as a young woman, that the Bubbe had died as she had lived, perfectly—that unlike her youthful mother's death, and her father's, her grandmother's death was natural, and no calamity.

The truth is that for women as well as men there are multiple plots that get braided. The marriage plot—the heroine's plot—is one among several. I wonder now: Did Reisel want to live in Ahzhe's house above the fancy grocery shop rather than in his parents' house above the bakery because (unlike his parents) he was a cosmopolitan modern man, selling Lindt chocolate and dried sweet fruits imported from the Middle East to his sweet-toothed neighbors instead of praying and swaying all day like a medieval Jew? Was she looking neither to immigrate to America nor to emigrate anywhere, but simply to escape her grandparents' ultra-observant way of life? When she begged her father to take her in, was she longing for love and protection and a proper home, or hoping to fashion a more modern life for herself outside the bakery?

Family history like all history is riddled and riven with prejudices: I grew up hearing about Ahzhe the feckless provider, the foolish father, the faithless husband and son—"the old whoremaster," in my violently orphaned uncle's terrible words. Not a respectable man, or a good one. But the lives of the obscure should be studied alongside other obscure lives—for instance, the parallel histories of their near neighbors. While looking into the truth of my mother's stories, I was introduced—with the kind assistance of a cousin, through the magic of the internet—to a different American family descended like ours from Mielecer Jews. One of them—a professor at a college, like me and my brother—helpfully sent me a recording of an interview with two of her elderly aunts that his mother had made years ago, which suggests another dimension or interpretation of my own mother's migration. Listening to anecdotes about people I had never heard of, in a mix of English and Yiddish, I was arrested by the sound of a familiar name.

"Ahzhe Thaler's store! Did I know it? Of course, everyone knew Ahzhe Thaler's store," one of the old aunts exclaims. Evidently, a room behind the fancy grocery store where Ahzhe sold *"Zuckerwaren, Delikatessen, und Sudfruchten"* was a secret gathering place for Jewish dissidents, especially Zionists planning to immigrate to Palestine. It was the favorite haunt of a cosmopolitan Mielecer who had been at the First Zionist Congress with Theodor Herzl in 1897, a man who attended Congresses after that. For the first time, I wonder: Did my mother seek entrée to a lively group of radical thinkers and dreamers, when she asked to live with her father? Life in sociable Ahzhe Thaler's orbit would have been freer, more exciting and interesting, than slaving to keep the oven burning, under Moishidle's rabbinical supervision.

What if Reisel's move out of her grandmother's house had nothing to do with the marriage plot? As I recall, my mother's Zionism was very different from my father's; in my childhood, his seemed to me more serious. His pride in the founding of the state of Israel sent him to Lake Success in 1948 to witness the moment when the Jewish state was voted into the United

Nations. Anxiously embraced after the Holocaust, my father's Zionism was focused on the formation of a safe, legitimate, and recognized Jewish state. In contrast, my mother had dreamed Zionist dreams as a girl in Europe. While he struggled with mastering a correspondence course that would enable him to enroll in a business school in Vienna—and prepare him for a lifetime of reading—she was singing and dancing the *hora*. Zionism, for her, was what secular learning was for my father. Her Palestine was his Paris, a personal version of the Enlightenment, a place to escape to from the Dark Ages and old-time religion, and from antisemitism. But she got to Israel only belatedly, as a tourist.

Many years later, when she told us about how much fun she had had in Hashomer Hatzair, she was in thrall to a dismissive husband who couldn't imagine that she—a woman with no education—could even have political views. She would present her life-changing Socialist Zionist meetings—or so I would conceive of them—in terms familiar to me, as a pretext for adolescent partying, the kind of *hora*-dancing Zionism I dallied with, looking for boyfriends at the Jewish Center in Queens during my otherwise too sober teenage years spent studiously at a girls' high school. But unlike me, whose parents encouraged a correctively "normal" American Jewish teenaged life in the 1950s, Reisel stole off with her favorite cousin Zanvel to hike and picnic in the hills and to dance and discuss forbidden Zionism against the wishes of her pious grandparents. From the Zionists she learned to rebel against religion—and her elders who loved her.

Although she dutifully raised her eyebrows, the way my father did, at the naïveté of credulous left-wing idealists and ideologues, she remained loyal to Zionism all her life—putting eighteen cents for luck in the *pushke*, hanging on the walls of her apartment ugly leather and silver artifacts handmade in Israel. She remained a faithful, even reverent member of Hadassah, which my father tolerated as a harmless organization that made *balebatish* American Jewish women feel important but also usefully supported a good hospital. Very late in her old age she surprised me by giving me a life membership in that organization. Publicly she mocked but secretly she admired her favorite sister-in-law Henia for her brilliant fund-raising exploits in the Pioneer Women, a Zionist women's group to the left of her own—a feat that got Henia named Queen Esther one year, and introduced to President Truman, and given a trip to Israel, all expenses paid.

Reisel was thrilled when in 1969 my father suggested that they themselves travel to Israel (she enjoyed the trip). He was even more excited: I can only imagine the pleasure he must have taken in legally leaving and entering not one but two modern civilized countries with an American passport.

# CHAPTER 5

# LOVE STORY

Time will say nothing but I told you so,
Time only knows the price we have to pay;
If I could tell you, I would let you know.

W. H. AUDEN

Happiness in marriage is entirely a matter of chance. If the dispo-
sitions of the parties are ever so well known to each other, or ever so
similar before-hand, it does not advance their felicity in the least.
They always continue to grow sufficiently unlike afterwards to have
their share of vexation; and it is better to know as little as possible of
the defects of the person with whom you are to pass your life.

CHARLOTTE LUCAS, in *Pride and Prejudice*

When I was a little girl, my mother's funny brother Sam—
Sammy, we called him—would visit her of a late afternoon after delivering a crate of eggs to a grocery store in our neighborhood in Astoria, before driving his little truck back home to
Brooklyn. He would come into the apartment making a lot of
noise and pick us up and whirl us around and mumble his plate
of false teeth in and out of his wide mouth to make us scream
with laughter. Sam would have been in his forties then. My
mother would serve him coffee and home-baked cake and they
would talk in Yiddish and laugh together—"Seriously, Sam?"
she would ask him—and after he left she would smile and then
shake her head sadly. From what I overheard, she worried that

Sam worked too hard, that his wife and children demanded too much of him.

He had assumed the burdens of a family man precociously, as a bachelor. I imagine him and Reisel together in 1925 or '26, strolling on the Lower East Side on a Sunday morning, both wearing hats. He was taking care of his greenhorn sister as he had taken care of his little brother in the orphanage during the decade or so he had lived in New York, visiting Harry regularly and making a point of giving him a proper bar mitzvah in a synagogue when the boy turned thirteen. He slipped the younger man a few dollars whenever he saw him, for years after that. A lively sister was even more fun than a little American brother: Reisel and Sam spoke confidentially, in Yiddish, and she laughed at his stories, recognized the people in them, and gave back as good as she got, conversationally. He was keeping company in those years with a dark-eyed American girl who also liked to laugh, and he was proud of having this merry sister to introduce to her.

As the brother and sister walked together for the company and the exercise, Reisel had been complaining about her bedroom with her new Litvak landlady, entertainingly, as was her way, but nevertheless complaining. Not only was the food bad there, both the bread and the tomatoes sliced paper-thin, but the woman, a very recent immigrant, had the nerve to correct her boarder's English. Reisel was beginning to get a firm footing as an American and a New Yorker. She already had opinions about the movies, and Prohibition, and the dashing mayor Jimmy Walker. Following Sam's instructions, she had been teaching herself English by reading the captions under the photographs in New York's Picture Newspaper, the *Daily News*. And this ignorant landlady had the gall to teach her the language! Reisel imitated her Yiddish accent: "*Doos is de flyor, doos is de ceilink, un doos is de vinder*," she mimicked, pointing first down, then up, and then across, as they walked on the sidewalk. "Also, Reisel *dahlink, meh zugt nisht* 'Good-Bye,' *meh zugt* 'Guh-Bye.'"

Sam threw his head back in appreciative laughter, then looked up to lock eyes unexpectedly with an unsmiling stranger walking toward them on the crowded sidewalk, an older woman he recognized as a Mielecer. It was of all people Git Lucius, my father's father Avrum Chayim Mayer's sour second wife, who instantly recognized affable Sam Thaler. She was walking with her daughter Rivka. In the "Erev Yom Kippur" notebook, my mother recalls the meeting:

One day I was walking with my brother Sam and we met Rivka and her mother. We were to become very good friends. So I moved in with them. That's how I met my Yussel. He arrived from France and I got kind of friendly with him. Took him to register in . . . a private school. I was already an American, took him places so that's how we got to love one another. I will never forget when he proposed to me. He said I have very little if we do get married and you or I will need something you will be the one to get it. I thought that was very sweet of your Pop and he was always very good and kind to me. My life with Yussel was good until we moved to Flushing and he got religious that's when things got not so good the first argument we had was in Flushing that was about 19 years after we were married. To be continued.

This is the last entry in the notebook. My mother either forgot about the book or misplaced it, or what she ended up writing caused her to lose interest in recalling the story of her life, which was not always the story of triumph it pleased her to tell.

I would have liked more details about the street scene she mentions. It has always seemed right to me that just as in a

Broadway musical—*Guys and Dolls*, say, or *My Sister Eileen*, *On the Town*, or *West Side Story*—the fateful encounter that determined the rest of my mother's life took place on the sidewalks of New York. As I imagine it, she and Sam easily got to talking and walking with the mother and daughter from their old hometown. As they walked along, Reisel keeping a sharp eye out for the prettiest dishes and trinkets for sale on the tables and pushcarts on the sidewalks and the streets, the two pairs of walkers eventually changed partners: the eagerly smiling young women got along well, and Git Lucius was eager to hear whatever gossip garrulous Sam could relate. Penny-pinching Git Lucius was interested, as well, in the possible prospect of a new but familiar young woman boarder, a decent-looking girl and a Mielecer. And Sam Thaler, thinking of settling down himself, told himself that Git Lucius—a Mielecer and an intelligent woman—would be like the mother she never had for his sister Reisel.

As for Reisel, who had just talked herself into leaving the room she was currently renting, she decided then and there to move in the following week for a couple of dollars less than she was paying the irritating Litvak landlady. Delighted to think of his sister safely off his hands and living in New York with a nice family, a Mielecer family, Sam sealed the deal, then celebrated by buying a piping hot potato knish for lunch for him and his sister at Yonah Schimmel's.

She would remain in that family for years, staying on for her own reasons after Rivka married and moved out. In the 1930 census she is reported by the US government to be living together with Abraham Chayim Mayer and his wife Gussie on Intervale Avenue in the Bronx: she is identified as the boarder Rose Thaler, a working milliner, the sole native New Yorker and English speaker in the household, as well as on that page. My father's name is missing from the census report.

What did she see in Yussel, what did he see in her, when they met in close quarters in a small apartment after their separate awkward moves west toward the modern world? Reflecting mirrors in each other's eyes (brown; hazel)? They came together in New York as *landsleit*, Galitzianers, Mielecers; they knew some of the same people in the old European home they both could recall nostalgically; coming to know one another was in some ways like a homecoming.

American born, she was as she saw it an old hand and an expert, by then, at navigating the city streets and subways, while he was brand new and overeducated and understood little English. But they both were strangers in a strange land, and in a position to help and comfort one another—and to make one another uncomfortable. Living together as if they were brother and sister in a family, the self-consciously superior young man and the energetic orphan must have fallen into one another's arms, eventually, for safety's sake—metaphorically, to begin with, and later really. Did both my parents-to-be—literary in their different ways—imagine their coming together was inevitable, as they say in Yiddish *bashert*, fated?

Not at the beginning, for sure. His special status in the household as a man and a son would have annoyed her: she had learned in her grandmother's house to be painfully sensitive to parental favoritism, and rivalrous with boys. At the beginning, she went out to work to pay her portion of the rent, and he did not. Then he managed to find work in a business owned by a Mielecer he knew. The job sustained him while he learned English—he registered at a language school—and got ready to go back to his studies. He was pretty good at retail for a shy and physically clumsy man, deploying his old-world politeness to please the *goyim* who came downtown to buy cheap, on Sundays, from Jews whose shops were conveniently open then as the uptown stores were not. His gentlemanly manners also usefully kept him at a comfortable distance from the coarse people he worked among. Eager to get on, he worked long hours, then read into the night.

Proximity threw him and Reisel together. There could not have been more than one bathroom; probably the toilet was down the hall. The pungent odors from Git Lucius's kitchen—onions and garlic, cabbage and fish—would have reminded them both of home; the apartment must have felt like an island of the old world in a confusing new one. The symmetries and the social structure were familiar to both of them: the overseeing parental landlords, rigid and observant and emotionally remote, and the grown-up children, The Missus's daughter Rivka and now The Mister's son—and over there Reisel Thaler, you know, Reisel, *Moishidles an einickle*, the poor relation, the granddaughter that Brucha Moishidles took in on her old age.

*Chez* Git Lucius, Reisel probably would have shared not only a room but a bed with Rivka. Of her very first days in New York, she wrote later that she and Sam "had to look for a job and a bedroom. The job I got from a Mielecer, and also moved in to them. They lived on Rivington St. We slept three girls in one bed. After they got to know me a little better they asked me to cut my toenails because I slept across from them in the same bed. So life went on until I decided that I did not like the job and my sleeping accommodation. I moved to another lady she was very nice I had a room all to myself. I paid $8 a month and worked uptown and was getting to be a real American." By the time she decided to move in with Rivka, she had already moved several times. Did she give up a room of her own, then, for the promise of pleasant company? And where did The Missus put The Mister's son when he turned up from Paris via Montreal? Did he sleep on the couch in the living room? Was there a living room, or a couch? Did The Mister's son and The Missus's daughter pay what Reisel paid for room and board?

Different habitats breed different habits, emotions, and notions and kinds of intimacy. The girls she slept with early on asked her to cut her toenails after they got to know her a little better: in the beginning, they slept together in one bed without knowing one another at all. Among kinds of knowing, where does not-only-sexual knowledge of the body rank, and in what ways is such knowledge acquired?

Reisel and Yussel would have been a little shy with one another, in the beginning; she was bolder than he was by nature. He was short and rather stiff, but she liked his looks. His clothes were odd—European—but she preferred dowdy to flashy. It was obvious that he thought he was her superior, but just as obvious that he preferred her to Rivka, which was not surprising, as she was better-looking, but flattering nevertheless. She valued his opinions, of which he had many, and he enjoyed her interest in listening to him talk. He was a man of the world like the Zionist organizers from elsewhere who had intrigued her in Mielec, years before; he had lived in Paris and Vienna and had dreamed of Jerusalem and Rome. He had read many books, and he kept on reading. But where did he read, in that cramped apartment, and when? Did The Missus insist he turn off the light to save money on the electricity? It is all very hard to imagine. Like her grandfather Moishidle, he was a scholar—but the books were different, secular. Both kinds of books were not for her, she took it for granted—she preferred a love story—but she respected them.

Without really deciding to make a project of doing so, she—a knowledgeable, knowing New York working girl—began to Americanize him. She advised him to follow Sam's instructions and learn English by reading the words under the pictures in the tabloid newspapers and figuring out their meanings, as she had done. He lowered himself awkwardly to do so—he made it clear that as an educated, thinking man he would much prefer a serious newspaper like the *New York Times*—but he stubbornly continued to pay for the course in English: he believed in school. She taught him how to find his way around the city—uptown and downtown, the subways and trollies and the buses, and the bridges and the parks, as well, and the best places to buy an ice cream or an onion roll. Walking beside her on the streets, he tried to match her pace and her quick takes on places and people, her confident sense of direction. Increasingly, he admired her pluck and her pleasure, even found them exciting.

George Eliot writes of the dairymaid Hetty Sorrel that she had never read a novel and therefore could not find a shape for her expectations: probably for the same reason, Hetty had little insight into the intricacies of character, and took no pleasure in language for its own sake, the way Reisel did—and Yussel, for all his bookishness, did not. (One of her grandsons remembers her taking him aside to ask him, confidentially, "Ezzie, tell me, what does it mean when you call something gross?")

Reisel's joy in a new or odd word or rhythm, a good piece of fresh bread, or a bright color was contagious. Trying to play her games and (in his view) win them, Yussel described to her in ponderous poetical detail, first in Yiddish but eventually in English, too, the broad vistas of the Champs-Elysées and the beauty of the lights on the Seine, at night. She seemed interested; she warmed to him, and he warmed back. Soon he turned into her teacher, making fun of her mistakes. She laughed: she liked it that he knew more than she did; it was fitting for a man, especially since he was only marginally taller. They went to the movies together, and she was a little jealous when the Francophile confessed how much he admired Claudette Colbert. She imagined the experiences with women he must have had in Paris. The two of them might very well have seen *The Jazz Singer* together. Perhaps the weirdest of all American Jewish immigration stories, it stars the Jewish actor and singer Al Jolson as the son of a cantor, who passionately adores his adoring mother and triumphantly becomes an American by singing onstage—in blackface!—in vaudeville a love song to his "Mammy" (!) instead of what he was meant to sing that night, his father's liturgical "Kol Nidre." The film, the first "talkie," capped the perverse wackiness of its story by being released on October 6, 1927, the evening after Yom Kippur, when Jewish audiences were back from the synagogue where they had repented for their sins—and free to go out to the movies.

In September 1929, Yussel went to register as a "pre-law" student at Washington Square College of New York University, and Reisel went with him. It was a disaster: "Josef Steuer" fled Washington Square precipitously, in a panic, when he was asked for his papers. In addition to his American-born girlfriend, he had brought with him the diplomas from the *Hochschule fur Welthandeln* in Vienna—but he had no passport, nothing from a nation-state that legitimized him by alleging he belonged to it. He could not register at NYU without such a document. In distress, ashamed of himself, he explained most of this to Reisel as they walked around and under the big arch in Washington Square; to cheer himself up, he described, in learned detail and at length, the punitive Ancient Roman policy regarding exile. Or at least I imagine he must have done.

A month or so later came another disaster: on Thursday, October 24, 1929, the stock market crashed, and although he had no stake in it, Josef Steuer crashed along with it. His hopes of an education and a profession were blown up and away. He had no idea what to do. The failed registration at NYU is the most vivid scene of the period as my mother described it. It shook her: he was terrified of being thrown out of the country, being sent back to God knows where.

In 1929 Americans were getting nervous about immigrants of certain dark and shady kinds, Jews for example, and Hungarians, Romanians, Italians, Roma. Reisel was embarrassed by Yussel's fear and his flight from Washington Square. In his place (but of course she was only a girl) she would have (charmingly) asked them what to do and done it, she must have thought. It was central to her view of life that a man should never be frightened: she scorned and pitied him. Probably that last was the fatal emotional step—Desdemona's. They became inextricably involved.

It was not until over ten years later, during World War II, that my father would leave his American-born wife and babies in their three-room apartment in Astoria to travel back to where he had come from, that is, to Montreal. Because this remained a family secret, I have no idea of what arrangements he—or someone—had made to change his immigration status. He stayed in Canada for several anxious days and nights, and returned with a Polish passport—he who could not speak a sentence in Polish!—issued on June 14, 1940, to "Josef S. Mayer." In the photograph he looks like a movie Mafioso. As soon as possible, he became what is oddly called a "naturalized" American citizen.

During those ten years, then for all his life afterward, he lived in terror of the authority of the state. In the 1930 census, he is not even listed as a member of his father's household. His immigration status threw a permanent shadow on the greater part of his working days, which he spent driving his car. Making an ambiguously permissible turn or parking within sight of a fire hydrant or (for a moment) illegally double-parking were risky moves for him. If for any reason he had to address a policeman, he always humbly, and more than once, called the man "Officer" to flatter him, infuriating me.

The work he finally devised for himself, first as a newcomer in New York and as it turned out for the rest of his life, was based on neither his intellect nor his education, but simply on his status as an undocumented immigrant and a Galitzianer Jew. Years later, he used to disparage people he disliked who worked in Jewish organizations as "professional Jews": he would cringe to hear me hang something close to that label on him. His business—many Jews like him were in it, at the time—was a modern variation on the stereotypes of both the wandering Jew and the moneylender. On the Lower East Side, he "dealt with" men who sold household goods wholesale—furniture, rugs, clothing, gold jewelry. Mostly "dry goods," sheets and towels. The lingua franca there was Yiddish: the wholesalers knew and trusted him. He bought from them and sold, retail, to his customers, "on time," that is, on the installment plan, years before Macy's offered its "layaway plan." The customers were working-class Queens housewives, mostly Italian American immigrants, who needed a new scatter rug or set of towels, or a small gold Bulova watch (made in Astoria) for a graduation gift. He packed up their purchases in brown paper tied with hairy string, then delivered them to small homes in Astoria, or Elmhurst, Maspeth, Corona, or Jackson Heights. Monday to Friday, he drove around collecting payments—and drove home to eat at his own table a lunch prepared for him by his wife. Sometimes, he let a customer skip a payment or two because he liked and trusted her. The women confided in him that they hoped their daughters would marry Jewish husbands, nice men like him who didn't drink or gamble or fool around, men who were reliable.

My father's General Motors car might have been a souped-up version of a peddler's cart, but his bookkeeping and his handwriting were elegant. I remember the long slim cards on which he kept his meticulous records—the part of the job he liked best. In my childhood he claimed to have an "office" at 44 East Broadway, but I never saw the inside of it: we sat in the car with our mother, double-parked and watching out for policemen, on the Sunday afternoons when he took us with him downtown. I recall those days as dark winter afternoons like the ones when we went to the cemetery in Ozone Park. I knew the peculiar names of the customers he talked about, but I never met any of them.

He was ashamed of being in his business, and I was too. I didn't like being asked what my father did and having to answer "businessman," as he instructed me to do. Was it one word or two? I asked him in annoyance. And couldn't he be a little more specific? Like, exactly what kind of business was it? I still have one of his yellowed cards in a drawer: "J. Mayer, Fine Clothes for Men, Women, and Children." I never saw him handle anything but towels. Sometimes I saw him writing numbers on the long manila cards that also read, at the top, "J. Mayer, Fine Clothes for Men, Women, and Children." On one occasion at least I heard him say he worked in dry goods, a cut above working in food, as it kept his hands clean.

I am harking back now to the period shortly after World War II, when Harry Truman was president—Harry S Truman, S without a period, because as Truman explained, S was his whole middle name, not an initial. My father repeated that to me. He signed himself "Joseph S. Mayer," explaining that unlike President Truman's his S had a dot after it because it stood for his middle name, Steuer, pronounced "Shtoyer." It turned out to be not a middle name at all but a former surname, which surprised me. When I traveled to London much later, he told me to look up some cousins on his mother's side, there, whose surname was Steuer. I did. They pronounced it "Styewer."

The truth about my father came out long after I grew up, when my husband applied for Conscientious Objector status to avoid the draft of doctors under thirty-five during the Vietnam War. The application required him to respond to government-issue questions about the citizenship of his parents as well as— surprising us all—the parents of his wife. The secret (it had ruined my father's life) was that he had lived uncomfortably in America as an undocumented alien from the late 1920s until 1942, when he left the country and re-entered it legally through the northern door he had come through the first time, Canada.

On reflection, it seems to me that my father's relation to the nation-state he lived in had been problematic and vexed from the very beginning of his life in Austria-Hungary—a peculiarly poignant burden for a man of his probity, rigidity, and allegiance to the law, a student of civics and history. Or perhaps the poignancy—and the ironies—developed during his life. Nature or nurture? History or politics?

Jewishness and the habit of observant Judaism, membership in a dispersed and despised migrant nation united by a language rather than a territory—a language that many of the people who spoke it considered a shameful, not quite legitimate language—was the central and determining fact of my father's life. Hidden from the state authorities from birth, constrained by concealment and impoverished frightened parents, not to mention those six hundred thirteen commandments that enjoined him to live apart and differently from any nation he lived in, he was a Jew above all. In the end, with more than a little help from changes in culture and public affairs, his childhood years in the *cheder* trumped his adolescent turn against religion, his embrace of modernity and Enlightenment in Vienna and Paris, his Anglophile studies of Edward

Gibbon's many volumes about the decline and fall of Rome, and even the energetic embrace of Reisel Thaler. Trying to live as he chose, he jousted always with a single windmill, a single irony. All roads, no matter how different and promising they appeared, led to the same place: Jewishness. He married for love, but the two moves he made with his wife managed to take him backward, not forward.

When I described my parents' move from Astoria to Flushing to my sociologist friend H., she wrinkled her nose and shrewdly asked whether my mother's richer friends' moves farther out on Long Island had "caused tensions in the marriage." It took me a moment to understand, but then I explained. Although they were busy with them all the time, my parents had no respect for material things. Regarding big-ticket items like houses, she deferred without question to my father as to what they could afford. My mother never aimed to be a "fency crecker": from her point of view, honest plainness was not only the best policy, but it gave her the moral upper hand. She loved to laugh at her rich brother Harry's address in Rockville Centre, a dead-end street called "The Loch," to which she gave the Yiddish, not the Scottish pronunciation (*loch* in Yiddish means not a lake but a hole). It wasn't the modesty of the little house in Flushing that ruined her marriage, I told H., feeling myself rising involuntarily, in my family's prideful manner, above mere material concerns: it was my father's foolish and vain entanglement with not one but two young American Orthodox rabbis in the new neighborhood.

In his fifties, at a high point in postwar prosperity, he managed to cash in some stocks and buy a little row house in a newly developed part of Queens—a former swamp. It must have been clear to him by then that this would be the acme of his worldly achievement: my mother recalled that at the very end of his life he told her he was proud of only two things he had done, marry her and buy the house. My brother and I were growing up and out of his orbit, by then, doing well by moving in directions he had only vague notions about. He had never had many friends: nobody seemed to him to be on his intellectual level except his eccentric bachelor cousin who had learned to be a furrier by reading, in the New York Public Library on Forty-Second Street, scientific how-to books about the treatment of animal skins. As he looked around the new Queens neighborhood for a synagogue for his son's bar mitzvah, my father encountered, for the first time in America, a man around his age whom he admired—also an immigrant and an observant Orthodox Jew. The two became good friends—and they dangled themselves and their European learning before not one but two new rabbis, competitors, both of whom were eager to build Orthodox congregations in the Jewish neighborhood. The rabbis admired my father's professorial style and his old-world learning. One of them was a scholar, "Modern Orthodox," with a PhD as well as a rabbinical degree; the other belonged to a rising group that called itself "Young Israel." "Mr. Mayer," as they called him, giddily toggled between the two, sometimes following and sometimes leading his new friend as the two of them fell hard for one and then the other rabbi.

Soon he found himself at war at home. He insisted for the first time that his wife and children observe the Sabbath and keep it holy: "Don't make the light!" he would shout at us, translating from the Yiddish, with a crazy righteous tyranny like Moishidle's. He was impossible to live with; old friends of my mother and his own relatives as well avoided him. In fewer than ten years, with us out of the house, he was seriously proposing to retire with Reisel to an Orthodox community in Israel, as his furrier cousins and their demented old father had done. She had to draw the line.

Reisel was obdurate: bad enough that she had had to move to Flushing. She had never liked anything there but the rock garden, she now claimed. Even though she had a horror of the heat of Florida, even as she proclaimed her single-minded patriotic love for New York, Reisel insisted that they move south instead of far away to the Middle East, saying she needed to be near her grandchildren, who lived in New York. The Jews of my parents' generation were all moving south: and she always did want to go in the same direction as other people.

Gregarious like her brother Sam, she needed people to talk to, people other than her husband, in addition to him, to admire her. And after his return to religion—and because of it—she no longer enjoyed walking and laughing with him as she had earlier. In fact, he was driving her crazy, she told me—and others as well. In the condominium just north of Miami, she would go into the walk-in closet some evenings and scream. She had married for love; she could never have imagined that it, that she, that they would end up that way.

At my friend L.'s daughter's white wedding on the Upper West Side in the early 1980s, the Catholic priest who officiated delighted himself by joking to a crowd liberally sprinkled with Jews that this was a mixed marriage, the bride having attended a Jesuit college and the groom a Vincentian one. In some sense every marriage is mixed, combining as it does different individuals and families.

Although my parents' marriage might seem more strikingly incestuous—joining together two people born into the same small circle, who had lived together for years in the same apartment, supervised by parent-surrogates—theirs was a mixed marriage, as well. He was the brains, as she reiterated, and she was the brawn. He was an intellectual, she worked with her hands. She was American born, an authentic Lower East

Side New Yorker like Al Smith, and a patriot, while he was a foreigner and an immigrant, a man used to the shadows. Although he became an American citizen in 1942, his accent, his manner, remained European Jewish.

More important were the consequences of their beginnings: she was proud of her native land, as she proudly called it, and he was afraid, intimidated by legal forms and the friendliest of policemen. And as he grew older, what she said became more and more true: afraid to work for or with other people, he became increasingly alone. He was scared of everything. Toward the end, he shone as a learned man in the synagogue, while she—always a lover of differences—stuck to her guns in her insistence on being democratic and ecumenical, extending her sympathies to all oppressed people.

She had been volubly outraged, as a young married woman, when Elaine, her once-a-week cleaning woman, had died of a heart attack on the sidewalk just outside the hospital in her Bronx neighborhood, where she had been (almost) taken for emergency treatment after collapsing in the street near her home. They had mistaken the young Black woman for a drunk, my mother repeated dolefully, convinced that the tragedy was caused by racial prejudice. She brought it up all her life as an example of the horrors of bigotry. She was proud of being against that evil: how could a Jew be otherwise? My father's views were a little different: his Germanic nineteenth-century insistence on the intrinsic differences between nations and races made him shy away from claiming, as she did, that all men and women were more the same than different. Fashions in clothing, he would explain pedantically, came downtown from Harlem: up there they had a sense of style, just as the French were good at fine cuisine. Different races had different talents and weaknesses. The Jews—the men, that is—were good at abstract thinking.

The innate and acquired social, political, and characterological differences between husband and wife—their polarization—increased over time: as Jane Austen suggests, and the puckish priest could not have known from experience any more than she could, every long marriage becomes a mixed marriage in its own way.

---

As a young woman I used to wonder whether, during their long engagement, my parents had slept together while living with The Mister and The Missus, and if so where: my mother was visibly embarrassed when she gave us the confusing dates of their long courtship, and she recalled that her girlfriends didn't believe her when she announced she was engaged. Now when I think of it, their secret seems to me to have more to do with money and immigration law than sex.

For starters, she had a paying job and he did not. And he never found a job commensurate with his abilities, a career. In spite of his intellect and education, in spite of his dignity and demeanor, in spite of the fact that he was a snob—or perhaps because of all that—he did the kind of work poor immigrants do: he worked for other immigrants at the edges of the economy. Literally. In the city where Macy's, on Thirty-Fourth Street and Broadway, was at the center of the trade in clothing and household goods, he worked "downtown" on the Jewish Lower East Side. He was ashamed of the work he did. She, on the other hand, had a more plausible working life, if a shorter one. Doing piecework for very low wages a few blocks from Herald Square, she enjoyed a sociable job that on more than one count—finery, audience, freedom, location—satisfied her sense of theater, and of herself.

The situation had to be reversed if the two of them were to

marry. She would have to quit her job, and he would have to support her: gender rules and roles were strict, for people of their class, time, and place. Although they had walked out together for privacy for years, they did not manage to marry until February 1933, nearly ten years after Sam married his dark-eyed sweetheart and very soon after the dressy wedding of Yussele and his much younger Russian bride, Henia. The Missus sourly criticized Reisel's diamond engagement ring: she didn't see why an expensive ring should be necessary. Either because or in spite of not being Yussel Mayer's mother, she was for them the paradigmatic Evil Mother-in-Law: she even managed to say or do something unforgivable—I think she brought photographs of her latest grandchild—when she visited the hospital after Reisel's first child was stillborn. Forgiving their relatives was a real problem for Reisel and Yussel both: they permanently hated Git Lucius.

Short, stubby people of no status in the world, my parents had in common a clear moral compass and an instinct to judge. In one respect they resembled Jane Austen's aristocratic Mr. Darcy: their good opinion, once lost, was lost forever.

---

In the years when she was working, Reisel couldn't wait to rush out of the house and go to work, mornings. But soon after Yussel arrived, she found she was also looking forward to going "home" at the end of the day, and to going out with him for a walk after a dull dinner. Yussel, for his part, amused himself by telling jokes and stories that made her laugh; he even tickled her, to hear her laugh. One evening, she told me, in a fit of the giggles, she tried to make him stop tickling her by saying his name, Yussel, and "Yunya" came out instead. This always sounded to me like a cleaned-up version of the story. In any case, for the rest of his life, that would be her pet name for him.

Did she marry him because he seemed familiar to her, yet another stranger-brother-cousin—a Mielecer, a Galitzianer, brought up in poverty and religiosity uncomfortably, as she herself had been, by Orthodox Jews, and struck in adolescence by rumors of the Enlightenment, or the Haskalah, or Zionism? Did they fancy themselves rebels and moderns when they walked out together Friday nights, and did he dare to light up a Lucky some eight or ten blocks from the no-smoking-on-the-Sabbath house? Was marrying him a way of not really leaving home and all its ambivalences? Could she have turned her back on her history and married someone who was not of her class and kind—the real-life cantor's son she had encountered with his family on board the *President Roosevelt*, for instance, or (not that she would think seriously of that for a minute) Eddie the tall Irish hat salesman who couldn't stop telling her how much he really liked her?

Abandoned by the mother who died and the father who didn't care, feeling threatened when her grandmother's health began to fail, she was a girl singularly alone in a world that was notoriously unkind to poor Jewish girls without protectors or money. But she was strong and sturdy and capable, up for it, up to it, whatever it turned out to be. She was cheerful, conscious of her luck in being American born, and in America. When rumors of the murder of most of the Jews of Europe, including her own beloved aunts, terrified and weakened her, she was grateful to have him at her side, a man of sterling character (as she proudly put it).

He read about what was going on in Europe in two newspapers a day, the *New York Times* and the *Evening Telegram* (but never the left-wing papers, as he claimed he already knew what the liberal line would be—and for that reason never ever the Jewish papers, either). He explained everything to her. He collected gold for the war effort and, as a member of the Blue Star Brigade, he sold war bonds with success, and was promoted to second lieutenant on July 8, 1944. He was a patriot, too. According to a lavish brochure in my files, he also served on important committees of the United Mielecer Relief, Inc., and although he contributed nowhere near as much money as some others, he was one of those honored at its Testimonial Dinner on May 27, 1945.

No matter how angry she got at her husband, my mother always insisted that he "had character" as, in both her view and his, most men and women did not. That tricky word is complex. She was proud of being, herself, a character, and proud of being gifted at the game of assuming different characters or roles in different circumstances. She enjoyed knowing she had a good reputation. But probably because she knew she was not as forthright sometimes as she might have been, she did not have the temerity to boast of *having* character, as she always said he did.

"Nothing so true as what you once let fall: / 'Most women have no character at all,'" Alexander Pope had written. Had she had the patience to read Pope, my mother would not have liked his coy argument that most women (except the one to whom he dedicates his poem, whom he gallantly credits with its thesis) are shallow and showy creatures, maternal and materialistic, mere "Matter too soft a lasting mark to bear." No, in her view women were tougher and smarter than men. But she would agree that most women worked hard at playing roles and had no sturdy authentic inner self, or backbone—and most men as well. My father, in contrast, had backbone, she insisted: he was "straight," as they both put it, as opposed to crooked (not gay). He was an honest and honorable man, and he did not try to seem or to be what he was not. (And by the way of course neither did she.) For her, this straightness of his was a function of his *having character*, which is not at all the same thing as *being a character*, acting out the social role of oneself. Even when she despaired of his timidity and clumsiness and raged against his unregenerate male tyranny, she honored and loved him for that.

Ocular proof of the successful Americanization and *embourgeoisement* of my parents—the astonishing reality of Reisel and Yussel become Rose and Joe—is provided by a group portrait of a portion of the extended Thaler family that was taken in 1947 by a professional party photographer in a hotel ball-

Descendants of Brucha and Moses Judah Thaler,
Washington, DC (1947)

room in Washington, DC. The occasion for the party was the bar mitzvah of my second cousin Harvey, the son of Yussel Liebes, whom my mother grew up with, and his wife Lena, who happened to be one of the two daughters of Ahzhe Thaler's second wife Paircha and her first husband. Dressed up for the occasion, my parents stare out proudly, benignly, tensely from a group of her close relatives, from behind their children, in the dark good looks of their *balebatish* middle age. I am the serious little girl of ten in puffed sleeves toward the left; my brother, seated next to me, is eight; it is a few years before our little family made the wrongheaded move from the melting pot of immigrant Astoria to Jewish Kew Gardens Hills, or Flushing.

I had never met the red-haired bar mitzvah boy, Harvey. They explained to me that he was my second cousin, the son of my mother's first cousin Yussel (now Joe) who had grown up with her in the bakery in Mielec—the creaky-voiced Yussel Liebes she always credited with baking the bread she carried with her when she left for America in 1924, the one who had perhaps (but probably not) thrown the hot cup of coffee that may have precipitated her voyage. I had never met him, either. Nor had I ever met my first cousin or half cousin Adrianne, who also lived in Washington—the long-legged, dark-eyed child who dangles from her father's arms in the photograph. And I didn't remember having met her mother, my mother's half sister Ruth or Roozha or Ruby, who has her hand on my father's shoulder in the photograph. (He must have hated that.) I don't think I had ever been to a bar mitzvah before—certainly not a gilded one like this—and I certainly had never been to Washington, DC, or indeed anywhere outside New York City—except for the Catskills, in the summers. I had never taken a train, except on the New York City subway. Most important, I—we, the big and little pairs that composed our still tight little family—had never slept at a hotel, as we had done the previous night and would do again the night of the party, all in the same room. My parents never tired of telling the story about—on, really—my brother, who had marveled too audibly as we entered that hotel room, "What a mansion!," I guess in front of the bellhop.

Talk about the mouths of babes. I can imagine the words in my mother's own head, in her vernacular: How do you like them apples, Rose and Joe Mayer and their two children in a hotel for two nights, for a bar mitzvah, a party! What luxury, what prosperity! The point was being dramatically made by Harvey's parents, who laid on the food and drink and live music for us: but we felt that, even though not rich like them, we were no longer *kaptzonim*, poor people. We went to restaurants for lunch as well as breakfast. We visited the awe-inspiring Lincoln Memorial and rode the elevator to the top of the Washington Monument while my own personal funny Uncle Sam pretended to get sick to his stomach and made loud bad jokes. And now here we were, ready to eat the fancy dinner at the party!

Uncle Sam and Aunt Yettie and their tall fair children, my cousins Sheila and Alvin, were frequent visitors to our home; so were my mother's cousins, Mike (Meilach Shifras in her stories) and his American wife Bertha, who, as my mother liked to recall, had snatched him up when she went to Europe to find a Jewish husband right before the war, when a man would marry anyone at all in order to get out. I was also familiar with strange German-speaking Naftali, called *der Nafti* by my jeering parents, and his dressy wife *die Rosel*, who came to dinner at our house. All these people belonged to the so-called "Family Circle" that sociable Sam tried to organize for years, which managed to meet a few times.

Big Mike with his athlete's carriage and loud baritone was the family hero: he had served in the US Army and spent a pleasant war in Nome, Alaska. *Der* Nafti and *die* Rosel were a different, tragic story: they had managed to get out of Germany and to New York just as Hitler was gaining power, just in time for Fred, their only son, to be drafted into the American Army. And in no time at all, in 1943, Fred had been killed in action in Italy, at not yet twenty. His parents' palpable grief made me anxious. The people at our table were all our relatives. Mike's wife Bertha and my aunt Ruth or Ruby wear orchids on their dresses that mark them as close relations of the bar mitzvah boy: they were his aunts while all the rest of us were only cousins.

The photograph and the occasion celebrated the prosperity in postwar America of the descendants of Brucha and Moishidle Thaler—that is, of those of their children's children who had managed to survive into nearly the middle of the twentieth century and had managed to snag and accept an invitation to the splendid party in the nation's capital. They included three of Ahzhe's six children, Sam, Rose, and Ruby; the Meema Shifra's son Meilach or Mike; and nervous German-speaking Naftali, the sad little furrier from Queens who had grown up in Germany and met his Mielecer relatives for the first time in New York. And, most importantly, although he is not in the picture here, behind this scene was Yussel Liebes, the son of my mother's favorite aunt, the cousin who might long ago have been sweet on my mother and who had in the event married her stepsister, back in Mielec. Which made my mother's evil stepmother and nemesis, Paircha, Harvey's real grandmother, the kind of authentic blood grandmother I never had. She was there at the party, and my father formally introduced me to her: she was tiny, dressed completely in black, with a wilting orchid pinned to her shoulder. Redolent of Mielec and death and the legendary past, in the flesh she was terrifying.

Yussel Liebes had begun to take over the Bubbe Brucha's bakery in Mielec years before she died; after the Bubbe's death,

Paircha had slid easily into the supervisory central role, her husband's mother's role. With her money as well as his in his pocket, with Paircha and two of her daughters, Yussel Liebes had immigrated to America in 1928. And the bakery, in effect, had immigrated with them. After a few years in the business in New York, where the first of his children was born, Yussel moved to Washington, DC, and opened his New Yorker Bakery—that is, Jewish bakery—there. By 1950 it was a thriving business, baking the tastiest traditional bagels and bialys and onion rolls, seeded and unseeded rye breads and braided challahs, honey cakes and sweet *bilkalech* for holidays. Its early customers would have been Galitzianer Jews homesick for New York and behind it the old country. But tastes changed over time. Ten or so years after Harvey's bar mitzvah, the New Yorker Bakery would boast of delivering to the White House.

By the time the war in Europe finally ended, the Thaler family of Mielec had endured many terrible losses. In 1937, just ten years before Harvey's bar mitzvah, one of my mother's uncles had described the deteriorating situation in Poland in a letter in Yiddish to a son who had managed to get to the new world. This is a translation:

> I have nothing of importance to write to you. You read the papers, don't you, so you see yourself what's going on here. It's too much to write. *The goyim* are buying up all the houses on the market square because Jews have no money. They've become impoverished because of the taxes they're paying. They're in fear of the *goyim*, who have been told they don't have to pay off the debts they owe to the Jews. So they don't pay taxes, don't pay off their debts, and on top of that they're all stirred up like wild animals, robbing and beating people up. I envy those who don't live in Poland. Only G-d knows what's yet

to come. [Someone] has already bought two houses on the market square, and the priest bought Israel Hermele's house, the one right in the middle of the square. In short, there's nothing left for us in Poland. *The goyim* are boycotting Jewish shops; young people have nothing to do. In secular schools, Jews are given a hard time. Young people have nothing to do, and older people who used to run good businesses are going broke. Our bakery is barely keeping afloat. Only G-d knows.

Many years earlier, in 1914, twelve-year-old Yussele Thaler, yearning to immigrate to America, wrote to his older brother Sam, who was already in New York. Writing in Yiddish, in Hebrew characters, on a postcard printed with the name of his father's fancy grocery, he complained that he had to get out of Mielec, where the *goyim* had banned people from patronizing Jewish shops. The situation seemed dire. In 1937 it was worse; soon it became impossible. The Thalers who remained in Mielec were all murdered.

Yussel Liebes took an only reasonable pleasure in showing off, in Washington, DC, in 1947, his wealth and bounty, his sweet wife and good-looking American children and, yes, his thriving bakery to the relatives who remembered him from his grandmother's bakery in Mielec. His achievement was real. With a little help from his wife and her mother, he had managed to preserve the Bubbe Brucha's bakery, to transplant it to America. After a few hard years working as a baker in New York, which his cousin Meilach Shifras also had done, he had opened his own shop in the nation's capital and enjoyed great financial success. His hard work and skill and devotion to the family's craft had preserved the Mielecer bakery and its breads, brown and gold, coarse and fine, sweet and savory. Through him the Bubbe's bagels and rolls and loaves—her Jewish bakery—had miraculously survived the Holocaust. As the owner and operator of the New Yorker Bakery, he was now in effect the head of the family. He was taking his role seriously, celebrating his success, by inviting the New York relatives he had seen only rarely in America to celebrate his son's bar mitzvah.

It was important to my mother and my father as well to attend the event together with their own promising American children, to show respect for Yussel Liebes's achievement as well as to show what remained of the Thalers and Mielec that, in spite of his higher education, Reisel's oddly aloof husband was not after all a *kaptzin*—and that the orphan girl the Bubbe Brucha had kindly adopted, the girl nobody else wanted, had become a respectable wife and mother, a good-looking American woman with a boy and a girl anyone would be proud of. The bar mitzvah that celebrated Harvey's accession to manhood more broadly also celebrated us, the American children of his Yiddish-speaking European parents and their nearly lost generation.

# CHAPTER 6

# PIECEWORK

Mister Harris, plutocrat,
Wants to give my cheek a pat,
If the Harris pat means a Paris hat, Okay!

COLE PORTER, "Always True to You in My Fashion" (1948)

I'm Anatole of Paris, I must design
I'm just like wine
I go to your head.

SYLVIA FINE (WITH DANNY KAYE), "Anatole of Paris" (1947)

*Starość nie radość.* (Old age ain't no joy.)

POLISH PROVERB OFTEN QUOTED BY MY MOTHER

Piecework is what my mother did as a milliner in New York in the 1920s. The term might also describe what I have done here, stitching together her stories about her life. In the millinery trade, a pieceworker was paid by the finished piece rather than by the hour; in the writing business—insofar as it is a business—the term suggests that the whole might be only the sum of its parts. I make this modest suggestion here for two good reasons: one, I only know some pieces of my mother's story; and two, in spite of recent cataract surgery I can't manage to see the whole of it clearly at once, only pieces of it, now with my nearsighted and then with my farsighted

eye, for which reason things seem by turns too close and too
distant.

Years ago, to people living outside New York, "New Yorker
Bakery" would have meant "Jewish bakery," but I'm not sure
it would mean that now. Words change their meanings as culture changes. Take, for example, the word "milliner." When
I tell people that my mother worked as a milliner, they get
some idea of her social class. But while the word would have
had that same effect two hundred years ago, it denoted something rather different then. In the early nineteenth century,
when Lord Byron disparaged the Lake Poets as insular and
low, he gossiped condescendingly, in rhyming verse, that
Coleridge and Southey had "followed the same path" when they
"[e]spoused two sisters, milliners of Bath," suggesting—with
lordly invidiousness—that the Fricker sisters were working-
class women. But he wasn't saying they made hats. In a modern
college text of Byron's *Don Juan*, a footnote usually points out
that the sisters who became those poets' wives made dresses;
the word "milliner" has become more specialized in meaning
over time, perhaps partly because hats were important mark-
ers of class in the nineteenth and early twentieth centuries.
What Byron was saying about class is quite clear, and of course
that's the gist of his gibe. By landing hard on the name of Bath,
the city the sisters came from, the rhythm of his verse may
have reminded readers of his time that the word "milliners"
derives from the English pronunciation of "Milaners," that is,
people from the city of Milan. The European trade in imported
feminine fripperies—ribbons, gloves, and hats—is at the root
of the word we now use exclusively of hat-makers. Its associations with urban working women continue to be strong.

The elaborateness of ornamental ladies' hats has been a butt
of social critics from the eighteenth-century English carica-

turists Gillray and Rowlandson through Danny Kaye and his wife and lyricist Sylvia Fine. Of course, silly hats are especially funny when they are in style. They have been, by fits and starts, over the years. In a letter to her sister, Jane Austen described the implausibly adorned ladies' hats she saw in Bath in the 1790s: "Flowers are very much worn, & Fruit is still more the thing," she wrote. "Eliz: has a bunch of Strawberries, and I have seen Grapes, Cherries, Plumbs, & Apricots." In New York City in the 1920s, when rebellious "flappers" cut their hair short for freedom's sake, hats were also all the rage—plain felt head-hugging cloche hats and turbans and perky little numbers worn at a jaunty angle, as well as large-brimmed straw hats loaded with ribbons and feathers and flowers and sometimes the fruits that amused Jane Austen.

From the 1920s through the mid-1940s, New York City was "the largest, the oldest, and the most important market in the country" for the millinery industry. Men and women of all classes wore hats out of doors—caps and hats, felt and straw, summer and winter. Cap-makers and makers of ladies' hats belonged to different labor unions. And while many frugal women made their own hats at home, relying on store-bought materials and patterns, most of them tried on and ordered and purchased hats from shops and, increasingly, department stores. Two out of three workers in the millinery trade were women. Most of them were trimmers; the blockers were all men.

Reisel Thaler arrived in New York in 1924 without the skills, education, experience, ambitions, looks, pretensions, and/or connections to qualify as, for instance, a clerk in an office, a bank, or a shop. The Jews she knew in New York worked at buying and selling either food or clothing. The needle trades were cleaner than the food business, and therefore more attractive. And the modernist vogue for short hair and head-hugging hats encouraged the hat market. For a girl brought up by religious women who wore wigs and babushkas to cover their hair, stylish hats would have been fascinating.

Hollywood stars and big retailers like R. H. Macy set the swiftly changing fashions in headgear. Advertisements in the newspapers suggested that working girls owed it to themselves to buy at least four hats a year; homemakers, who went out less, were encouraged to purchase at least two. Hats sold for $1.50 and up: by 1937, the largest volume of hats wholesaled between $7.50 and $13.50 a dozen, and there were more millinery workers in the city than the producers of hats could absorb. "Little milliners" claiming a connection to Paris tempted rich women to pay much more for stylish confections designed to set off a particular shape of face, to frame a unique personality.

Lilly Daché, the little milliner who made it big in hats in New York, claimed to have disembarked in that city in 1924, the same year my mother did—in her case straight from Paris. Later, rumor had it that she originated in Vienna or an obscure place farther east: the classic idyllic French country childhood she describes in her memoir, *Talking Through My Hats* (1946), is so very general and familiar that it might well have been made up of whole narrative cloth, in Hollywood.

Lilly surely did some work in self-fashioning as well as hat-making in the years before she came to rest on her laurels as a name brand. The larger story she tells is the fantastic stuff of early twentieth-century legend: a beautiful but virtuous young woman, a poor immigrant with talent, comes to America alone with no money or connections, eludes all manner of snares, sees in a window a sign saying "Milliner Wanted," and (after an obligatory stint at Macy's) sets up shop on then-fashionable upper Broadway. Because she is beautiful and gifted, diligent and good, she achieves success in the Land of Opportunity. She finds another good young woman to be her roommate, enjoys the company of an unimportant male admirer or two, but for the most part lives and works chastely, on her own.

In the conventionally structured life story Lilly tells, it is no less than William Randolph Hearst who launches her to stardom—by ordering one of her hats as a gift for his mistress, Marion Davies. Her subsequent customers include Mary Pickford, Marilyn Miller, Marlene Dietrich, and Merle Oberon (one story has that star bringing home her new hat in a convertible taxicab with the roof open to accommodate it). Finally, she finds true love and marries a rich French businessman who has made a fortune in (what else?) the beauty business. In her book, Lilly Daché writes that she would have gladly stopped working had she and her husband been lucky enough to have children. It is a success story of the period, made as if for the movies—or made by them, and then enacted by Lilly Daché.

Among the many immigrant women in New York who sewed for a living before readymade clothes made their jobs obsolete, there was a hierarchy. Seamstresses did the simplest, most basic work, sewing pieces of cloth together by running up seams on machines, often in sweatshops. To be a dressmaker who pinned and tucked and followed a pattern required more skill and talent, and it was a big step up, economically and socially. Dressmakers like milliners often worked in their own homes, but some of them sewed together side by side in small factories. At the top of the heap, in the needle trades, were the imaginative, artistic designers. It was all women's work. As a girl in Mielec, my mother had learned some domestic skills from her grandmother and aunts, including sewing with both a needle and a machine powered by a treadle. And she was, as she boasted, handy.

Writing about his odd choice to work with his hands as a chemist in a laboratory, the Italian Jewish writer Primo Levi describes it as a break with "an ancient atrophy of ours, of our family, of our caste," that is, of educated middle-class Jewish men from Turin, in the Piedmont area. "What were we able to do with our hands? Nothing, or almost nothing. The women, yes—our mothers and grandmothers had lively, agile hands, they knew how to sew and cook, some even played the piano, painted with watercolors, embroidered, braided their hair. But we, and our fathers?" The same extreme gender difference characterized my mother's very different, also Jewish, family and caste. Following the wonder rabbi's advice, the Bubbe Brucha had used her hands to knead bread to ensure there would be food on the table for Moishidle and the children. A girl who pleased a prospective mother-in-law by being good at untying knots would also be good at knitting, crocheting, and sewing, all of which my mother did enthusiastically, all her life.

The first job Reisel landed in New York was, inevitably, as a seamstress, but soon a landlady's daughter found her a less onerous and repetitive and better-paying job in a factory that made ladies' hats. She was hired as a trimmer. In no time, as she liked to tell it, a kindly Black man—she doesn't say where or how she met him, but he is a variant on a recurrent figure in her stories, a benign fatherly older man, not a Jew, who is impressed by her girlish charms and helps her—advised her that she would do well to look for similar work uptown, where the factories were more airy and the pay was better than it was on the crowded Lower East Side. She jumped at the chance to move up.

Trimmers in millineries in New York, back then, were for the most part young single women newly arrived in America. Their job was to do the finishing touches that made a hat distinctive, for instance to take a head-hugging body and a brim, if there was one, and tack onto it the ribbons, veiling, and braid, the beads, felt flowers, and jaunty feathers, that gave a hat its style. If you were handy and happened to have an eye and a flair, this was the job for you. Reisel enjoyed it. The work was congenial—the "girls" sat companionably around a table, and there wasn't too much noise from machines to prevent chat. She enjoyed gossiping about the boss and sharing confidences with her coworkers, learning about their lives outside the factory, and guessing about the secrets they didn't reveal. There were women of all ages, from different places, grim Communists from Russia and volatile Hungarians and even a girl from South America. There were beautiful Italian girls and plain old maids, women who thought they were too good for the work and others who feared they weren't really up to it. Reisel loved the variety and the company.

It was irregular work, seasonal, fashion-driven, and very low-paid. There were a lot of jobs in the hat business, but there were even more poor women—mostly immigrants, but some American girls from big poor families—who sought to fill them. Many of them preferred piecework, which meant being paid by the finished piece rather than drawing an hourly salary, and their employers found it profitable, as they could let such employees go after the season. Fast, sociable, energetic, and competitive, Reisel enjoyed racing the clock, and beating the other girls. Learning the differences among materials and how to handle them, and their names—chenille and chiffon, georgette and gingham, buckram, organdy, and braid and tulle and voile—interested her; and knowing how to recognize and identify their different looks and feels made her feel smart, authoritative. She liked fashioning a felt flower that made all the difference to a little brimless hat, and she was dazzled by the increasing variety of readymade trims that could transform a basic turban or a cloche into a thing of beauty in just minutes of clever stitching. Piecework meant you were paid by the hat: it encouraged artisanal pride. I remember her in her productive old age, scrunching up her eyes and holding

something she'd just made at arm's length, assessing it criti-
cally, admiringly.

She enjoyed telling us, decades later, that her hats were
often sent back to her to correct, the pieces having been too
hastily and loosely stitched together: in her later years, she
rather boasted of this. Being fast at household tasks was not
exactly a marketable skill, but it was her skill and she took
pride and pleasure in it. It worked for her, in the millinery
trade. In no time, she became, as she put it, "a crackerjack"
("creckerjeck"). Not only the owners and other operators but
also the salesmen who took the hats out into the world praised
her speed, and one year some of them chipped in to buy her a
present because they had made so much profit because of her
fast work. The girls liked her too: they elected her forelady of
the union, and when she finally got married they had a party
for her with a huge cake, and bought her a wedding present.

In his interview with her, when Gabriel tries to get her to talk
about the Depression, she says over and over that it was hard,
then, for my father to get a job. "And you, Grandma? Did you
have trouble finding work?" the interviewer insists. She evades
the question, either because she (unlike her husband) had in
fact had no trouble or because she refuses to admit she ever
had any real trouble or—or and—because she has forgotten
that part of her life, having never told a story about it, which
would have been the kind of sad story she had no time for.

It was my mother's nature to compete, and to want to be in
style, to go with the flow: doing that easily was part of what
she liked about living in the city. Her urge to conform drove
me crazy when I was a young teenager. My gorge used to rise
in sympathetic fury, along with my father's, as I sat with my
brother in the backseat of the car, Sundays, while we wobbled
at one or another busy intersection. We two couples, big and

little, were driving from Queens—my father was doing the driving—to visit either his father or brother in the Bronx, or one of her two married brothers (Sam and Joe) and their families in Brooklyn. *"Geh, geh vie alle cars gehen"* ("Go where all the cars are going"), my mother would urge, pointing energetically toward the windshield, as the car moved very, very slowly into dangerously merging traffic.

She enjoyed explaining to just about anybody that the car knew how to go to visit my father's customers. That my father had no control of the car or any other tool or implement delighted her. A *Luftmensch*, he couldn't throw or catch a ball; she had had to instruct him, more than once, in the mechanics of opening a can. And he had no sense of direction, while she had a good one. He agreed with all of this, congenially. All his assets were intellectual, impractical, superior, and she admired them. But her inclination was always to go where all the cars were going; his was to find his own way. Working in the millinery business—in fashion, in her fashion—had suited her. She had loved it.

---

Toward the end of a long life that had been mostly safe, settled, and sedentary, the story of her return to America came to seem extraordinary and marvelous, even to her. Certainly, it seemed wonderful to her grandchildren as they listened to the talkative cheerful old lady who—unlike, for instance, their bookish mother—had been so heroically adventurous, as a girl, as to pick up and move across the Atlantic Ocean alone, on her own. And imagine if she had *not* gone to America when she did, how terrible that would have been! It was consoling for her, even inspiring, to recall her youthful confidence and eagerness, her imagination and hopefulness. But on the other hand her voyage back to New York had also been overdetermined, by her parents' history and her own. Her brother Sam had gone back to New York when he was seventeen; her brother Yussele longed for years to follow him; and Hinda, a bold girl around her age whose mother had married Ahzhe Thaler, was planning to go at just about the time that Reisel was making her plans. People came back from America to Mielec reporting that there were opportunities in New York. She had family in New York, two brothers. Hinda also found a job in the needle trade. The promise that engaged the Greene Kuzine was out there to propel a brave girl forward.

Trying to imagine my mother as a young woman on her own in New York in the Roaring Twenties, before she decided to marry and settle with my father on the other side of the brand-new Triborough Bridge, I picture her strolling down a crowded street in midtown on a hot summer day, walking east and north from the West Thirties to eat her lunch in Bryant Park. She is holding a long, flat beige leatherette purse—not yet called "vegan leather"—in one hand and, in the other hand, wrapped up in a brown paper bag, the egg-on-an-onion-roll sandwich she had prepared for herself that morning. Under the little brim of her chic cloche, her keen eyes search for anything or anybody worth a second look.

I imagine her in a long narrow skirt with a slit on one side, her feet in flats but then, on second thought, low heels. The same lines are fashionable again, now. Admiring her youthful elasticity, I find myself annoyed by her jaunty stride—and yes, the contrast with my arthritic progress in telling her story. I am overwhelmed by the limitation that that lithe young woman of years ago unknowingly imposed on her biographer, the gaps in the record, the lack of information about the interesting nine or ten years she spent on her own in New York

Reisel Thaler, New York (ca. 1927)

City, doing piecework in a millinery factory. I turn away as she finishes her sandwich and folds up the waxed paper, putting it in her purse to use again, and leans back on the park bench to get sun on her face—as she never ever would do, for fear of the sun, sixty years later in Florida.

How can I know what it felt like to be Reisel Thaler back then? Why did she say so little that was substantive about that interesting part of her life? Except for mentioning the odd friend she made there—and later lost touch with—she refused to talk about her working life: asked about the place where she had sat sewing hats, she deflected the question and explained that Mr. Gilbert's place was called The Gildor because his wife was named Dora. I wonder idly whether, aside from the companionship, it was unpleasant work. For some reason— annoyance about my ignorance is a part of it—I am suddenly in a big hurry to finish up her story, to discover what it's about. Irritated by both of us, I recognize that I'm feeling too much like my mother, who was always in a rush. I know now, as she also came to know too late, when she was old, that this is a bad mistake. So let me try to slow down and take my time.

I close my eyes again to focus on her taking the sun on the park bench in the middle of the city in the middle of the work-day, in the crowded green space between Sixth and Fifth Avenues, not far from what they used to call the crossroads of the world, Times Square. Not too many years before my mother came to sit there, there had been a reservoir in the space behind the Public Library: in my childhood, my great-uncle Harry, my mother's uncle on her mother's side, who admitted he had voted Republican only once, for Theodore Roosevelt, had talked nostalgically about that beautiful reservoir. In the 1920s, the trees that had been planted to shade the benches were still slender. The young woman who would become my mother was comfortable on her break from work, enjoying the crowded public place and her own temporary anonymity: a working girl without a home or even a room of her own seemed, was, just as good as anyone else in the streets and parks of the big city. Proud of her smarts and her strength and her stylish outfit, proud to be far above Clinton Street on the Jewish Lower East Side, she was excited by all the heterogeneous people, delighted to be on her own and many miles from her too observant aunts and uncles in Mielec, free to jump or run if she wanted, or even to whistle. (Jews didn't whistle, or so they claimed, but all her life, with a finger hooked into her mouth, my mother could manage a piercing two-note whistle.) She was even free to chew gum, as Americans did.

She was conscious of being only blocks away from the awesome high-ceilinged cathedrals of retail on Fifth Avenue, with their toney names: *Lord* and Taylor, *Best* and Company, Saks *Fifth Avenue*. Rainy days, she might stroll through one or two of the ground floors of those great stores, on her lunch hour, and browse among the lavish displays, maybe even pick up a handbag to stroke the leather and examine the stitching. Contemplating the colorful bottles of scent on a counter, she would be annoyingly reminded of Yussel, her uncertain suitor or maybe a sort of cousin and not a suitor at all, who told her once—she was telling him about a Valentine's Day gift one of the girls at work had received from her boyfriend—that to give a lady perfume suggested she smelled bad without it. Was he making a bad joke, or did he really believe that? Was he jealous of the boyfriend who bought the girl a gift—as she herself had envied the girl? Was he insisting that Reisel take him quirks and all, or trying to push her away?

Silly to think of him here, on her lunch break in Bryant Park: why was she wasting her time doing that? She squints up at the blue sky, deciding to stay on her bench and look at the people walking past her, singly or in twos and threes, purposefully for the most part and with a midtown dignity. This wasn't a neighborhood where people actually lived, and the street life was stately rather than revealing: everyone was from somewhere else, passing through the world's crossroads, putting their best foot forward.

She could pick out the different kinds of people: the Irish and the Italians and the different kinds of Jews, bearded Orthodox men in black from the diamond district nearby and Americanized women from high-class families in their best summer dresses; she could identify some of the languages, Polish and German and Russian and Yiddish and Hungarian and the occasional odd clang of Chinese. There were tall blond men who looked like they must be Swedes, and darker ones, American Indians and Negroes. She had seen her first Negro as a little girl in Mielec after the war, a lanky milk-chocolate youth in a khaki American Army uniform. He was giving out chewing gum to all the kids, chewing meanwhile himself, and he flashed her a big smile as he gave her a stick. It was her first chewing gum: she made sure to throw it away before her grandparents could see it. "My Ma gave me a nickel, to buy a pickle / I didn't buy a pickle, I bought some chewing gum. O chew chew chew chew choongum, Do I love choongum. . . ." She loved that song, sang it to keep cheerful, held on to it for years: turns out it's a tune with African roots, a tune that Gershwin incorporated into the score for *An American in Paris*. A simple tune, endlessly repetitious, that evokes the mindless optimism of 1920s New York, and—for her—would have neatly connected the smelly wooden pickle barrels of the Lower East Side with the exotic smiling soldier.

Almost a whole century before Reisel sat in the sun on her bench in Bryant Park, the young poet William Wordsworth came down to the city of London from the calm and orderly cloisters of Cambridge and, before that, the green hills and blue lakes of his native Cumberland. In his long poem about his life, Wordsworth listed the kinds of people from elsewhere he was excited to see on the streets of the great metropolis, representatives of a wider world than he had known. Their heterogeneity exhilarated him: he was, he wrote,

> . . . well pleased to note
> Among the crowd all specimens of man,
> Through all the colours which the sun bestows,
> And every character of form and face:
> The Swede, the Russian; from the genial south,
> The Frenchman and the Spaniard; from remote
> America, the Hunter-Indian; Moors,
> Malays, Lascars, the Tartar, the Chinese,
> And Negro Ladies in white muslin gowns.

The Negro Ladies were showstopping; you had to look again, to spell it out in black and white, to stop time as they passed, as in a movie, joining together different worlds.

It was a different era. Months before she boarded the ship in Bremen, Reisel's brother Sam in New York had written a letter to President Harding (and/or to his wife) and yet another letter to the State Department, explaining that his young sister, an American citizen, was about to cross the Atlantic alone, and pleading for his protection. He kept the replies with his important papers all his life. Returning the copy of Reisel's birth certificate that Sam had sent, a Second Assistant Secretary of State wrote back that while the department was "not in a position to provide an escort for your sister, an instruction will be sent to the American Consul General at Warsaw to render her such assistance in this way as he may find possible and proper." A letter from another factotum, typed on White House stationery, advised that "Mrs. Harding appreciates your natural anxiety for your sister" and helpfully suggested that Reisel should consult the consul in Poland. "It may be possible that he would know of agencies over there such as our Young Women's Christian Association or the Travelers Aid, who would be able to give your sister the protection you desire for her," the writer airily conjectured. Or he might go to the headquarters of the Travelers Aid in New York "or some such organization, who might be able to inform you as to whether they have agencies abroad." The pronouns "our" and "they" separate the writer from the Jewish recipient of the letter. It is dated June 21, 1923: it took nearly a year to make the arrangements for her journey.

It made some sense for Sam Thaler and Mrs. Harding's secretary to be or to appear to be concerned about a Jewish girl traveling alone, who was likely to get ensnared by so-called White Slavers: a generation earlier, journalists had published scandalous stories about the involvement of the Orthodox Jewish community with criminals who supplied South American brothels. Round-heeled Galitzianer girls still figured, then, in trashy books and plays and jokes. It was brave of Reisel to come to America alone as she did, and her older brother's solicitude made sense.

My mother never talked about how lonely and scared she must have been at least some of the time in those early years in the city, how anxious about what would, what could, what might happen to her. She had great innate confidence about managing a girl's ordinary life, could handle herself when a man paused in front of her bench, whether he was a leering gent in a straw hat or a working man in a cap, strolling through the park on his lunch hour, sniffing around the girls. No problem for her to read an open face or look away firmly from the other kind. She knew how to deflect or correct a flirtatious move with a reminder that we are all of us brothers and sisters without designs on one another. Four brothers and a host of admiring male cousins had encouraged an easy relation to the other sex, and eventually a dim view of sex and gender.

Did she ever, in those years, as Gabriel once asked her delicately, have a fella? She twinkled but quickly decided she wouldn't say. From a remark she made to me when I was in the throes of my first misguided sexual relationship—"they all know how to feel you up," *tapn* in Yiddish—I suspect she must have had one or two. But it was her boast and her creed and her story that my father had been the only man in her life. And one of the things she taught me is that claims to narrative authority demand respect.

The few good stories she told later on about those years were mostly about the people she met in the millinery business— the girl who always sat next to her, who came back from her lunch break, one day, and with a lavish theatrical fling of an arm invited Reisel to "touch the hand that touched the hand of Rudolph Valentino"—an event that must have taken place early on, as Valentino, the sexy Sheik of Araby, died in August 1926, after a tour to publicize a second Sheik movie. And there was the one about the beautiful Italian girl who had talked her way into getting a job in the shop but, once seated next to Reisel at the sewing table, tearfully confessed she had no idea what to do with the packet of felt and ribbon and veiling they had given her. Fast Rosie showed her on the spot how to fashion the bits and pieces of stuff into a wearable hat, generously giving up time that she could have been converting into money for herself. Solidarity with other working women was natural, for her—and it was in the air.

She loved to repeat the story of how she handled brusque Mr. Braizel, the boss to whom she had said "Good morning" every day for years without getting a response—until one day she didn't look at him and he said, in distress, "Ross," and she imitated his foreign accent, "Where's your 'Good morning'?" Mr. Braizel was the boss she terrified when, having been elected the union forelady, she was persuaded to call a stoppage after he insulted one timid girl, who had burst into tears: "Ross," he pleaded with her, in his foreign accent, "you're killing the business for everyone, it's the season, you don't call a stoppage for that." Rattled, she took his advice and sent everyone back to work. She had been delighted to be elected, and to be in charge. She was thrilled to belong to the union, and she admired the activist Rose Schneiderman, an immigrant like herself (Schneiderman had gone to school in Chelm). But reflexively she deferred to men.

It was the men in the hat business—the blockers and the makers of caps—who had persuaded the "girls" to unionize in the first place; from my mother's point of view, they were—being men—as unlikely as the bosses to be a working girl's natural allies. She liked the idea of a union for the same reasons she liked socialism—the idea of all kinds of people united in the face of oppression—but growing up in the Bubbe Brucha's household had made her suspicious of ideologies. She flirted with socialism and feminism, but she was personally unprepared to go out on a political limb. It was hard for her to take herself seriously, in this area. Indiscriminately sympathetic and much too easily impressed, she could always see the truth of both sides of an argument. She was quickly persuaded by Mr. Braizel's appeal, and by his authority and experience; she had no trouble finding his practical view of the issue reasonable; and she immediately retracted her rash order to her troops. Of course, she loved it that Mr. Braizel had had to plead with her: it was payback for caving in.

Working alongside some ten or twelve other immigrant women at a long table in a loft in the West Thirties, walking on the crowded streets and riding the subway, she learned about men and women and politics and power. She looked around; she drew conclusions. She liked learning the things other people knew, and she chose intimates from among her savvier coworkers. Once she told us about going down to Greenwich Village with a girlfriend, where they noticed, in a restaurant, another pair of girls who seemed excessively absorbed in one another: when they themselves moved on, they linked arms and gaily said, "Les-be-on our way," feeling excitingly sophisticated. She loved the slang of the period, the trendy one-liners and puns: "She's a nice girl, in her way, but she don't weigh much," she would remark years later, baffling people who didn't hear the pun. Did she ever go to nightclubs to listen to jazz? Did men take her drinking in speakeasies? A glass of champagne to celebrate a graduation or an anniversary made her dizzy, in my time, so probably not. People change, however; and apparently the saintly Bubbe Brucha tippled a little. Once when my mother was in her eighties, I was driving her through midtown and somehow got lost in the narrow side streets near the Port Authority, where women I was beginning to call "sex workers" lounged in dark doorways. I pretended not to notice them and made no comment: in my fifties, I was embarrassed to confront sex directly in the presence of my mother. She was cooler: with a glance out her window, she murmured as if to herself, "Now that's a terrible job."

About sex and gender, my mother, in her old age, was programmatically "liberal," as she put it. One summer evening after dinner in Vermont, when my sons were in their early twenties, she told them a story about her youth in Mielec that went like this (I ran upstairs and wrote it down):

There was a man, yes, even in Mielec there was a man like that, he was a very religious man, and he was married to a woman, she was just like a man. She had a voice like a man, she dressed like a man, she looked like a man. She would go to *shul* with him. People said he should divorce her—in Europe it was easy to divorce, they didn't get married by a judge, they went to a rabbi, so to divorce you went again to the rabbi—people said he should, such a religious man, but he didn't, he lived with her. They would go to *shul* together. And he would sit next to my grandfather in the *Beth Hamidrash*. And one day, the man said to my grandfather that I shouldn't be sitting there with the men, that I should be in the women's section. I was a big girl already, eleven, twelve years old. But my grandfather said, "She's with me, she sits here, it's my seat." Oh, they were nice people, my grandparents, you would have liked them.

The subject on the dinner table evidently had been sex and gender roles, and my mother was coming on characteristically as a consummately modern and hip old lady. Her anecdote worries the traditionally important distinctions between men and women, and adults and children. I'm not sure exactly what she meant to say by telling it: that people have always been peculiar as well as blind to their own oddities? That sexual matters were as complex and as vexed as they are now, back then in Jewish Mielec, in Eastern Europe, not very long after the end of the nineteenth century? The story is also nostalgic and an attempt at magic: the teller wants to bring back her good grandparents, to show them off as more flexible that you might have thought, to introduce them with pride to her grandchildren.

What did she do as a working girl when she wasn't working? She went to the movies, with girlfriends and with my father. With or without him, she saw *The Jazz Singer*, starring Al Jolson as the cantor's son who sings of his "Mammy" in blackface, but although I tried hard to find out, I have no idea of what she made of it then or later. She would speak with awe and special authority, as if she had known them, of movie stars before my time, John Gilbert and Jean Harlow, Lillian Gish and Miriam Hopkins and Greta Garbo, John Barrymore, Pola Negri, Gloria Swanson, Norma Shearer and Douglas Fairbanks Jr., Billie Burke and Myrna Loy and Leslie Howard. She liked to repeat the joke she always attributed to my grandfather The Mister, about the little man who sells you the ticket to the movie but is no longer there when the movie is over so you can't complain it was no good and demand your money back. I can't imagine her making that rude demand, and I guess she couldn't imagine The Mister doing so.

In the summers she must have gone to Coney Island, where she lay on the beach and went on the rides with her friends, boys and girls together. I know for sure that she never went to the Millinery Center Synagogue on Sixth Avenue, just across the street from Bryant Park, because the place was not built until the 1940s, when New York was full of woeful refugees and rich Jews seeking to do something for them. Having come to America for freedom *from* religion, Reisel would not have gone in even if the building had been there.

Her circle of immigrant girls and couples was limited, and (although she did like meeting famous people, later on) she had few social ambitions. Her quest, I think, was for enlightenment—if not exactly The Enlightenment. She loved the variety and multiplicity of the city, was curious about the differences among kinds of people, how they talked and how they lived. Since my mother's funeral, I have not visited her grave on Long Island: for me her spirit resides in the green rectangle of Bryant Park, alongside the much more imposing but also comic spirit of another American Jew, a woman born a generation before her, Gertrude Stein, whose bust (by Jo Davidson) stands serenely beneath the trees there. She had a calm, sure sense of herself, as my mother also had.

One of the few good things that happened to my mother in her old age—good partly because it lent itself nicely to her ongoing comic narrative of her life story—was a chance encounter on a Saturday morning with a stranger who stopped her and my father as they walked to the synagogue in Hallandale, north of Miami, where they then lived. (My mother hated "that stinkin' Florida" for the same reason she had hated Flushing: the barrenness of the streets and sameness of the people, the boring couples ridiculously pleased with themselves to have landed there, the fact that the whole neighborhood was—she quoted her Russian sister-in-law Henia—"*nyekulturni*.") The man on the street introduced himself as a Mielecer and a former intimate of my father, whom he had known years before when they were young men in Paris working together in the featherbed factory. Always less than gregarious and visibly fading by then, my father said very little, and to move things along my mother told the man they were in a hurry, on their way to *shul*: my father had thoroughly re-embraced Orthodox Judaism by then, and in a combination of sadism and terror forced her— she hated it—to walk with him to the synagogue every Saturday. The man laughed loudly, satirically. "Look at that, Yussel Mayer!" he jeered. "Going to the synagogue! Well, I guess that's the way it goes." To annoy my father, before walking away he asked him whether he still remembered Paris, where the two of them had gone out together to eat *chazar* and dance with *shiksas*.

I can't imagine that my father said anything at all, but my mother relished recalling this meeting, which proved that my father's return to religion, in late life, was inconsistent and inauthentic, as well as very inconvenient for her. She was proud that, unlike him, she never changed her mind once she made it up: and she had no use for religion. Although she understood his motives for it—growing old, getting more and more scared of death—she hated his late-life embrace of rabbis and syna- gogues and strict observances. Embracing all that, separating himself from her, he had become a ridiculous domestic tyrant. Slipping easily into her repertoire of comical anecdotes, the story about the man who had known him in Paris almost re- paid her for her husband's having forgotten—deliberately, in her view—his years of freedom and fun and apostasy, and for the weekly torture she endured, when he was old, of going with him to *shul*. Almost but not quite.

Also, she had for years been envious of his adventures in Paris, before he met her: she had not shared them, but they had lent him the worldly polish, the rakish hint of rebellious- ness, that had seduced her in the first place.

But she didn't, she couldn't really, complain—except obliquely. She prided herself throughout her long life on hav- ing made the right choices. To hear her tell it, she had done her work well, indeed brilliantly, in the millinery business. At home, she could hem a skirt or sew on a button faster than you could slip off a garment and hand it to her. She liked to recall her successes, the girls in the union who liked to laugh with her and elected her forelady, the salesmen who bought her a cake because she had finished more hats in a shorter time than any other girl on the floor—more profit for them, as well as her. (Small potatoes, on both sides: in 1937, by which time she had quit the job, most trimmers like her in the millinery trade earned less than $300 a year.) She appreciated talent and beauty, and admired the clever designer, even though the poor thing was an old maid, and the beautiful Italian girls, and even—because they were so odd—the intense Russians who had come to America after the revolution. It was through them (she wanted to learn more) that she had met the clever and elegant little Henia, whom she fatefully introduced to her brother Yussele—big mistake—when he finally arrived from Europe (with an American passport). It was one of Henia's married Russian friends who had named her child Lenin: my parents—they knew her as a couple—never stopped laughing about the time they overheard her say in Yiddish, putting the little boy to bed, "*Lenin, gay pish sich oyss*" ("Lenin, go piss"). My father adored that story.

My parents didn't tell sad tales, at least not to us children, whom they sought to protect from evil; and they only wanted to hear good things from us. Like my mother, I tend to shy away from pain and tragedy, and I am often rude to people who seek to savor the details of someone else's disaster. One day recently, contemplating my cousin Alvin's Family Tree, I realized for the first time, with a shiver, why the aunts Sheindel and Feige, who were Brucha's daughters every bit as much as Shifra and Liebe were, and resident in the bakery and helpful in raising my mother, fail to figure in her stories: it's because both of them were murdered by the Nazis, along with their husbands and children. She would tear up and stay silent for long minutes if somebody mentioned either one of those dead women's names.

To hear her talk about it, nothing bad had befallen her in her independent New York years, although she was alone in the city with only a distracted brother or two to protect her. She was no Sister Carrie. Her stories were all about her speed and diligence and her success, her triumphs and her pleasures, her charm. She was glad to be in New York, in America, her own, her native land. She was not a snob like my father, but as an American born she considered herself superior to mere immigrants. She worked hard, in America, at having a good time with her hard-earned money, and at getting the education that had been denied her. She read novels in English, went to the movies, talked to people, and looked around. The millinery floor, the series of families in tenements that she lodged with, and the streets of Manhattan were—as Ishmael in *Moby Dick* says of the whaling ship—her Harvard College and her Yale. She was surprised, in a restaurant, to find that the eggplant she ordered had nothing to do with eggs: she was embarrassed, and told the story on herself, but also (she had a nerve!) on the illogical English language.

My mother lived on her own in New York City from March 17, 1924, until she married my father, although for the last seven or eight of those years she was involved with him. I have little evidence of those years, only a very few facts and dates and photographs and a small number of anecdotes. I piece them together here as if into a quilt—or a hat, to top my tale. Here are some more fragments.

On her sixty-fourth birthday, my mother telephoned to let me know how very strange it felt to be so old: she'd looked in the mirror and marveled: "Look at that, Rose Mayer, sixty-four years old." I told this story then to my friend M., who like me was thirty-six years old at the time, and we laughed at her. When we ourselves turned sixty-four, we recalled it to one another, remembering that to us it had not seemed strange at all for Rose Mayer to be that old, while to her it was astonishing, as our own great ages now were to us. Living the story is different from telling it.

When I imagine my mother in the act of being my mother, I see her in her nineteen-forties pompadour with its gray streak; I can also picture her much later as my children's grandmother, sitting in a folding chair in Vermont after a walk up and down the green hills, describing the layout of central

Mielec to them, naming the stores around the marketplace; and she haunts me as the dazed wreck of herself in her last year of old age—look at that, Rose Mayer, ninety-three years old!—when she was still clear-minded but increasingly isolated and suspicious. In other words, when I try to conjure the woman I think she really was, I see her not as the motherless toddler or the hearty member of the Zionist youth group I never knew, back in Poland, but as a full-time mother in Astoria, in Queens, in her vigorous forties, cleaning the house and cooking and baking and gossiping about her neighbors and sisters-in-law, proud of being exactly who she was and saying exactly what she thought—of being herself. She liked it that people admired her for it.

*Starość nie radość*, the old Polish woodcutter had repeated to the Bubbe Brucha: there is little to enjoy in old age. Reisel's husband and her brothers and sisters-in-law all predeceased her, except for Henia, who continued to bustle in Brooklyn, still connected to people she knew. Her two best friends Mrs. W. and Mrs. K., who had lived in our apartment house in Astoria, had dropped out of her life soon after they moved "out to the Island" with their husbands, the doctor and the lawyer. My mother's intimacy with these artificial ladies had always mystified me. In Astoria, she had also cultivated a friendship with the much younger and prettier Teddy, who also lived in the building, and also had a husband with a mustache, as Mrs. W. and Mrs. K. both did. Lively Teddy dyed her hair blonde—which in my mother's view was something nice women didn't do. Teddy flirted, at least, with being a less than respectable woman; and my mother enjoyed watching, evaluating, and judging her goings-on. She made a point of calling her "Tessie," allegedly her "real" name, to lend her some needed authenticity.

It was Teddy I overheard calling me a *klutz*, under her breath, after I stupidly steered my sled down a hill and into a tree, under her supervision, and banged myself up. I never forgave her for that. When pretty Teddy fell in love with the darkly handsome bachelor on the second floor, who to look at was a more sober version of her husband Murray (a real dummy, according to my mother), Emma Woodhouse could not have been more engaged in the goings-on than Rose Mayer was. Many years later, she was vague, to me, about exactly what had happened between them, either out of loyalty to Teddy, whom she lost touch with, or perhaps because she never allowed herself to know.

My mother needed people to talk to and talk about: she collected people, as Jane Austen, in a famous letter, suggested one does before beginning to write a novel. Characters were what interested her, and character. She was fascinated, for instance, by earnest, dull Sarah Cohen, the mother of a classmate of mine, who was a native of Burlington, Vermont, and a college graduate, and had (as my mother put it) a sister a lesbian. She was flattered by Sarah's interest in her. When in second or third grade Sarah's daughter informed me that masked robbers had come into their house through an open window in the night (they lived in a small house in Astoria, not an apartment in a big building like ours), and I believed it and told the story to my mother, she related this to Sarah, and Sarah laughed and remarked that her daughter had "an imagination." Imagination, indeed, my mother snorted—to Sarah and to everyone else she knew. The girl was a liar, plain and simple. And her mother, shockingly, was encouraging her to lie. It was wrong.

She was a harsh judge of human nature. "What do you need her for?" my mother would say about a friend (like Sarah's daughter) who had disappointed me, when I was sad about losing her as a friend. For years I theorized that it was Henry James who helped me recover from having had such a mother by explaining it was wrong to use people as instruments. My mother didn't think there was anything wrong with that: she used other people to maintain her sense of self (and her sense of humor). In Kew Gardens Hills, she made few friends: by then her children were too old for their parents to befriend one another, and since she avoided the social life of the synagogue sisterhoods there was nowhere for her to find new friends. Those were the years in which we encouraged her to learn to drive, or to take a course at a local college, which she refused to do.

After my father died, she lived alone in the apartment in "that stinkin' Florida," where the colorized framed photograph of the Bubbe Brucha hung in the living room and the bedroom was filled with the set of French-style American-made furniture my parents had bought when they married. She was comfortable but bored by her life, and loved to fly north, away from it. I have a note from my mother written in ballpoint pen on lined paper, dated July 11, 1987, with "July" crossed out and "I must be in a hurry I mean June" scrawled next to the date. "Rachel dearest," it goes. "Thank you for making the reservation for me. All is well. I called for the boarding pass. It will wait for me when I get to the airport. I am really looking forward to see you all. Here it is getting warmer. I take my walk early in the morning. Go to the pool in the afternoon. That's what I call a hard life. What do you think? Love to you all, Mom."

In those Florida years, she relied on two new best friends. Al was a retired New York City cab driver, who took her where she wanted to go in the neighborhood of their condominium, at a reduced price: he adored her. And Isabel, who was crippled and bitter and (no one should know from such a thing) had no children, who lived on the same floor of the apartment house, would drop by every evening, after supper. Isabel had harsh opinions, political and social. My mother would listen to her astute criticisms and niggling complaints about this one and that one and try to cheer her up, in vain. And when Isabel would finally leave for the night and close the door behind her, my mother would lean against it and say out loud to the walls (my son Ezra told me years ago she told him), "Fuck you." Now in his fifties, so many years after his beloved grandmother's death, Ezra repudiates the story. Maybe she said, "God damn her," he tells me now. "But not that." But I am sure he told me the other word. Remembering our lives and telling our stories, as we grow older, we flatten the people around us as we complicate ourselves. My mother always explained, in defense of her difficult friend, that Isabel "had qualities." She couldn't specify what they were.

Her brothers' daughters visited her when they came to Florida, and they left her apartment with booties and/or sticks of *mandelbroit* (usually one stick of each kind) that they could slice up and serve to their friends at home. She talked on the phone long distance to Harry's wife Rae on Long Island and to Henia in Brooklyn once a week or so, and there were a few younger neighbors—kind women who remembered her from Flushing or had met her in Florida—who checked in on her. Over time, the old Jews in her Florida neighborhood were "dying out," as she put it, and being replaced by newer immigrants from farther east, as they had been in Flushing. I remember meeting a couple of middle-aged Bulgarians who had moved into an apartment on her floor: they were charmed by her. Always interested in the exotic, she reported to me that they spent most of their evenings watching television while snacking on raw garlic cloves for their health. They amused her, but she sadly repeated to me on the phone that "there was nobody to talk to." (She also used that expression, in Yiddish, to describe—delicately, she thought—a dull person who didn't interest her.) She tried hard to make friends with my Buffalonian mother-in-law, who was also widowed and lived nearby, but that lady's lack of a sense of humor was an obstacle. They were an unlikely pair, although roughly the same age. When Kate complained in public of being old, Rose would reiterate merrily, encouragingly, in Yiddish, that she was aging like a good wine (*"Azoi vie a gitteh vahn"*), drawing out the last vowel and causing poor Kate, who couldn't tell whether she was being laughed at, to go bright pink in confusion, which gratified wicked Rose.

Then one day, as she told it, she took an egg out of the refrigerator and—she couldn't explain it—it was an egg and it wasn't an egg, and somehow, she didn't know why, she dropped the egg, and she decided she could no longer live in Florida alone.

———

The giant square quilts my mother made for me in her old age are stored in our damp house in Vermont in the trunks the boys took to summer camp with them some forty years ago. There are two big ones with a lot of orange in them, fit for a king-sized bed, and three small ones. Making quilts like that must have been a craft project that caught on for a time in some neighborhoods north of Miami, but I have never seen another quilt like mine. My mother made them by hand, using six-inch squares of brightly printed cotton fabric sold in packets at a local "notions" store: there are a lot of poison oranges and greens calculated to pierce through the fog of cataracts. She would fold each square into a triangle, fill it with cotton batting purchased for the purpose, and sew it together as if she were filling pockets of rolled-out dough with sweet cooked prunes for *hamantashen* for Purim. Then she sewed two triangles together into squares, and ultimately pieced all of them together into a quilt. Seated and sewing quickly by hand, she let the growing quilt pool at her feet.

When used even lightly by sleepers, these coverings, from the start, turn into clumsy nets of holes; they are uncomfortable, heavy without being warm. During the summers in Vermont, she would spend many hours with a needle and thread, repairing them; colorful but not beautiful, with scratchy seams on their undersides, they are hard to find a use for and hard to throw away.

What remains of the dead? Do you throw out your dead father's worn-out underwear as soon as possible, to save the remnants of his dignity? What do you do with your dead mother's "trousseau"? My mother carefully preserved and toward the end gave me two garments to which she gave that fancy French name. She somehow conveyed the idea that she had worn this silky underwear on her wedding night—a bias-cut slip and matching loose panties that close at the waist with a little button and a tiny loop. Did she in fact wear them once, then beautifully launder and iron them, and wrap them in tissue paper so that they still look unworn? Nothing like my size, the color of high-end smoked salmon hand-sliced super-thin, the garments lie undisturbed now, rolled up in a towel in the back of a drawer in my dresser.

My mother turned ninety in 1995. In the fall of that year, sending out Jewish New Year cards as usual, she scrawled on her card to my son Daniel, "I also want to thank you for your letter which I did not answer. Please excuse me. When a person is 90 years old, things don't go as fast even [as when] you are 85. Life is getting a little harder, so what? No complain. As long as I can still take care of myself."

She came to Vermont as usual in the summer of 1995, after turning ninety. I can't remember whether I picked her up as usual in Burlington, that year, or if that was the summer I had to find her at a little airport in New Hampshire on the Fourth of July, smaller than I remembered her and shaken by having been the only passenger on the very little plane she had had to take from New York City. Was that the summer she sported a button that read "Better Gay than Grumpy," to the delight of all the young people in the village? It must have been earlier, when she sat on the couch watching baby Ben crawl on his belly across the living room floor and philosophized, to the horror of the baby's mother, "Soon he'll be walking, then running, then he'll go to school, and then he'll be off to college." Old people tend to see time collapsing all around them. And my mother had always been in a hurry, as she had been when she beat out the other girls at piecework.

When I drove my mother north toward Montpelier on Interstate 95, she would look around and softly, reverently murmur, "purple mountains majesty." In fine weather she would walk every morning "to Amadon," which was the name on the mailbox near the top of the hill, where she turned back. It was all uphill to Amadon, and she carried a stick. She walked alone as fast as she could, exercising for health, but it was a pleasure, not a task for her, and she enjoyed it mightily. When Peggy Potter, who lived maybe a hundred yards beyond Amadon, hospitably invited her to come by for a cup of coffee after her walk up the hill, some morning, she was flattered, but she never took her up on it: she liked Peggy fine, but she also liked her walk the way it was, the climb uphill followed by the easy descent toward the little white church at the crossroads, then up on the gravel to our house to rest. The last summer, she didn't manage to walk regularly.

When she went back to Florida in August, that year, before we drove her to the airport, she said goodbye to everyone she knew in the village in such a way that everyone knew she was thinking she wouldn't be back. I put it down to her irrepressible sense of drama, at the time. I don't want to remember her last lonely months in Florida, or her final frantic months in New York. She died at ninety-three, in the Jewish nursing home on 106th Street in Manhattan. "When I kick the bucket," she used to say. "When I'm pushing up the daisies." With a little giggle of disbelief. As if.

---

I want to end my version of my mother's story—since I have the luxury of choice—by picturing her in the summer of 1992, sitting on a not-so-comfortable chair in our living room in Brookfield, Vermont, watching Bill Clinton and Al Gore accept their party's nomination for president and vice president. As the two men smile and wave on the small screen of the flickering black-and-white television, she smiles back happily, *kvelling*. They spoke to her directly, as Democrats and as men, just as Jimmy Walker, Al Smith, Fiorello LaGuardia, and, from a loftier place, Franklin Delano Roosevelt had done. "Two such handsome boys," she marveled. She did not lament their lack of gravitas. She was on their side and she loved them, separately and together—and not at all blindly. She registered, and lamented, Al Gore's stiffness, suspected Clinton's too-easy charm, and recognized Clinton's mother as not quite a respectable woman. But Hillary impressed her. After my mother's death, I found among her papers a clipping from a 1993 issue of the *Miami Herald* about the mother of Janet Reno, Clinton's attorney general, who was very proud of her daughter.

There's no place here for the sad stories of what happened later to these once powerful people and to the idea of democracy, to my mother and to the values of fairness and honesty she had lived by and for: her enthusiasm for youth and hope and boyish good looks, her naïve, wrongheaded, pie-eyed faith in the future, in America, was what had kept her going.

# 2021

"Piecework" might be an even better metaphor than I thought it was, I found myself reflecting the other day. Being paid by the piece—by the hat, in my mother's case—encourages artisanal pride, as I have written. To contemplate a long life as a series of pieces, to hold each one at arm's length and squint to assess its worth, might be better, certainly more comfortable, than trying to figure out what the whole thing adds up to. You might say to yourself, for instance, that that choice, investment, decision, or dinner party was not such a bad move, after all. But lives break down into such very different kinds of pieces; and it doesn't do to lean too hard on metaphors. What a piece of work is man, and woman too. Better to reflect on stories.

This morning my half grapefruit turned out to be full of those shriveled little slippery seeds you sometimes find there, and as I struggled lazily to spoon them aside, I found myself recalling my mother warning me, in my childhood, that if you swallowed a seed by accident a grapefruit tree would grow in your stomach. Memories tend to sabotage you. I would have heard that less than likely story for the first time some eighty years ago.

It would have been some forty or fifty years later that a student in my freshman composition class, in a "personal experience paper," recalled her mother's putting the same unforgettably ludicrous tragicomic idea into her childish head. My student's mother was "an uneducated immigrant from China," she wrote, and the grapefruit tree story was meant to illustrate maternal ineptitude, and the foreignness and all-around weirdness that had made the daughter feel, well, abnormal, among her non-Asian peers in New York.

After I shared my identical personal story with her during our private conference, my student and I chatted a little about grapefruits and grapefruit spoons, and then, waxing sophisticated, about cross-cultural commonalities among what are sometimes called old wives' tales (*bubbe meyses*, or grandmothers' stories, in Yiddish), and about parents who scared and scarred their children without meaning to, and children who were too young and literal-minded to understand the parental tone of voice.

It was not until many more years later that I heard about my friend A.'s late father, also an immigrant but neither from Mielec nor China, who had soberly advised her, when she was little, that those shriveled-looking tiny seeds in grapefruits are full of vitamins and good for you.

But that is altogether another story, as my mother used to say.

# ACKNOWLEDGMENTS

My thanks first to Daniel Brownstein, for his inspired and intrepid research and his sympathetic imagination; to Alice Kaplan, for her readerly brilliance and discerning encouragement; and to Ann Peters, for her generosity, tact, and keen editorial eye.

I am very grateful as well to important others: Gabriel Brownstein and Marcia Lerner, for (among other things) recording my mother's memories and having them transcribed; Pat Brennan and Alan Mayer, for finding the book and for the erudition; Alice Kessler-Harris, for the conversation and the support; and Ezra Shales, for lovingly recalling and cannily emending.

Thanks, too, to these old friends and first cousins for reading and advising and/or helping me to connect some dots: Susan Thaler Abramson, Adrianne Blue, Myriam Chapman, Doris Friedensohn, Helene Foley, Elisabeth Jakab, Sheila Thaler Pekar, and Alvin I. Thaler.

For help with the Polish and the Yiddish, my thanks to Eve Jochnowitz, Agnieszka Legutko, and Paula Teitelbaum.

# NOTES

1 Chapter 1, p. 5: See Larry Wolff, *The Idea of Galicia: History and Fantasy in Habsburg Political Culture* (Palo Alto, CA: Stanford University Press, 2012), p. 402, citing Daniel Soyer, *Jewish Immigrant Associations and American Identity in New York* (Cambridge, MA: Harvard University Press, 1997).

2 Chapter 1, p. 18: On Jewish surnames, see Wolff, p. 29.

3 Chapter 1, p. 20: Joseph Roth, *Report from a Parisian Paradise: Essays from France, 1925–1939*, trans. Michael Hofmann (New York: W. W. Norton & Co., 2004).

4 Chapter 2, p. 41: Paul Kriwaczek, *Yiddish Civilisation: The Rise and Fall of a Forgotten Nation* (New York: Random House, 2005).

5 Chapter 3, p. 73: Rochelle G. Saidel, *Mielec, Poland: The Shtetl That Became a Nazi Concentration Camp* (Jerusalem and New York: Gefen, 2012).

6 Chapter 4, p. 93: Anthony Trollope, *The Prime Minister* (1875–1876), chapter 37 (Oxford and New York: Oxford University Press, 1977), p. 350.

7 Chapter 6, p. 151: Jane Austen, Letter to Cassandra, 2 June 1799, *Jane Austen's Letters*, ed. Deirdre Le Faye (Oxford and New York: Oxford University Press, 1995), p. 42.

8 Chapter 6, p. 151: *Primer of Problems in the Millinery Industry, Bulletin of the Women's Bureau No. 179* (Washington, DC: US Department of Labor, 1941).

9 Chapter 6, p. 153: Primo Levi, *The Periodic Table*, trans. Raymond Rosenthal (New York: Schocken Books, 1984), p. 24.

10 Chapter 6, p. 163: William Wordsworth, *The Prelude* (1850), Book VII, ll. 220–28; *William Wordsworth: The Major Works*, ed. Stephen Gill (Oxford and New York: Oxford University Press, 2000), p. 474.

11 Chapter 6, p. 175: See Jane Austen, letter to Anna Austen, 9–18 September 1814, Le Faye, ed., p. 275.